A PORTRAIT OF PAUL

'GOD AND LIFE' SERIES

A PORTRAIT OF PAUL
J. ALEXANDER FINDLAY, M.A., D.D.

LIBERAL PURITANISM
A. W. HARRISON, M.C., B.A., B.Sc., D.D.

THE PRESENT MESSAGE OF THE
PARABLES
R. E. ROBERTS, D.D.

INTERPRETERS OF LIFE
ROBERT STRONG, M.A., B.Litt.

WHAT I BELIEVE
Edited by B. AQUILA BARBER
A Symposium by Eminent Ministers and
Laymen with an Introduction by the Editor.

THE HEAVENLY OCTAVE : A STUDY
OF THE BEATITUDES
FRANK W. BOREHAM, D.D.

METHODIST GOOD COMPANIONS.
G. ELSIE HARRISON, B.A.

HAVE FAITH IN GOD.
NORMAN H. SNAITH, M.A. (Oxon.).
Senior Kennicott Hebrew Scholar, 1925.

THE WHITE PATH. SKETCHES AND
STORIES
MARGARET DOREEN HADDON.

DO THE TEN COMMANDMENTS
STAND TO-DAY ?
J. PARTON MILUM, B.Sc., Ph.D.

THE DISCIPLE WHOM JESUS
LOVED.
Lectures on the Fourth Gospel.
W. F. LOFTHOUSE, M.A., D.D.

A PORTRAIT OF PAUL

By

J. ALEXANDER FINDLAY, M.A., D.D.

Author of
Jesus as they saw Him,
Jesus in the First Gospel,
What did Jesus Teach? &c.

LONDON
THE EPWORTH PRESS
(Edgar C. Barton)
25-35 CITY ROAD, E.C.1

First Edition April, 1935
Second Edition, July 1936

Made and Printed in Great Britain by the KEMP HALL PRESS, LTD.
in the City of Oxford

'In piam memoriam patris mei
apostoli Pauli studiosissimi.'

PREFACE

I SHOULD like to acknowledge my indebtedness to two students and friends of mine at Didsbury College, Messrs. R. H. Copestake and K. C. Forrester, who have very kindly revised my proofs and prepared an index of Scripture texts. My other obligations are mentioned in the text and foot-notes.

J. ALEX. FINDLAY.

Didsbury College,
    Manchester.
       March 1935.

CONTENTS

SUGGESTED ORDER OF THE EPISTLES

    I. Thessalonians (to the whole Church at Thessalonica).
   II. 2 Thessalonians (to its Jewish members).
  III. Galatians.
  IV. Romans (Chaps. i–xv).
   V. 2 Corinthians (Chaps. vi, 14—vii, 1).
  VI. 1 Corinthians.
 VII. Philippians (Chaps. iii, 2—iv, 3).
VIII. 2 Corinthians (Chaps. x, 1—xiii, 12).
  IX. 2 Corinthians (Chaps. i, 1—vi, 13 ; vii, 2—ix, 15).
   X. Romans (Chap. xvi, 1–23).
  XI. 'Ephesians.'
 XII. Colossians.
XIII. Philemon.
XIV. Philippians (Chaps. i, 1—iii, 1 ; iv, 4–23).

Genuine parts of the Epistles to Timothy and Titus written at various times during Paul's missionary journeys.

INTRODUCTION

It is fashionable in some quarters to set Jesus and Paul in opposition. Jesus was, it was suggested, the lover at once of children, flowers and sinners ; Paul looks at the sunlit world about him with gloomy eyes, sees Nature ' groaning and travailing in pain,' and seems only interested in sinners when they are actual or possible members of the Church. Jesus told stories about fathers and sons, masters and stewards, shepherds and sheep, and the lives of the poor; Paul talks about ' the law,' ' circumcision,' ' justification,' abstractions which mean little or nothing to us ; Jesus spoke of the Kingdom, Paul of the Church, and so on.

There is some truth in such comparisons, but they are fair neither to Jesus nor Paul. Jesus was far more interested in religion than in the pageant of outward life about Him; if He took and used with matchless ease and artistry the sights and sounds of the countryside or the common ways of men and women as illustrations they were always ' parables,' that is, they were selected as suggesting something or Someone *beyond themselves*. And, though Paul is the townsman as truly as Jesus is the countryman, he too had a keen and eager interest in the stir and rhythm of life about him. His very theological terms were the commonplaces of the exchange, the law-court, and the slave-market, and even words like ' circumcision,' ' the law,' represented burning questions of social and international relationship.

A more serious charge against Paul has been to the effect that he developed the simple teaching of Jesus, concerned with the fatherhood of God and the brotherhood of man, into a rigid and abstract theological dogma.

But the teaching of Jesus is not by any means simple, while Paul's theology is neither as abstract nor as complicated as some treatises on ' Paulinism ' would suggest. In any case, two at least of the Synoptic Gospels—sometimes extolled at Paul's expense—were written under his influence. This is certainly true of Mark's Gospel, the earliest and simplest of the three.   The very first words of that Gospel, which may be rendered ' This is where the gospel about Jesus Christ began,' bring before us a word (' gospel ') which Paul had made part of the vocabulary of the Church. It is doubtful whether any of our Gospels would have been written, if Paul had not created the constituency which demanded them.   Certainly, if he had never done his work, the books which might have been written would not have been at all like our Gospels ; we have Paul to thank for them.   The First Gospel, it is true, contains within it a tradition independent of, if not directly antipathetic to, Paul's influence, and the Third seems curiously indifferent to his master-ideas, when we remember that it was almost certainly written by an intimate friend and companion of his, but both accept the general Marcan scheme, a scheme dictated by the evangelist's purpose, announced in the plainest way, to illustrate *the doctrine of salvation* through the Cross and Resurrection of Jesus as preached by Paul.   In spite of their Semitic sources, they are Greek books for Greek-speaking people, and these people the members of Paul's Churches.   The Gospels and the Epistles indeed explain and supplement each other.

It is desirable that the shallowness of this antithesis between Jesus and Paul should be exposed, for it seems to the present writer that there is a serious lack of sympathy between the evangelical scholar and most of the people for whom he should be thinking and writing on this matter.

Most scholars of this generation, as of the last, consciously or otherwise, test the value of different strands in the Synoptic Gospels by their consonance with Paul's doctrine of salvation ; this seems to be true whether they are High or Low or Free Churchmen, whether they are German or British or American.   Scholars arrive at their explanation of Paul's gospel of salvation and go on to assess the value of everything else by its measure.   On the other hand, less critical but more widely-read writers of religious best-sellers still concentrate upon the Jesus of the Gospels with little or no reference to Pauline interpretations.   These books are neither so clear-cut nor so well written as the others, but the fact that they sell so much more rapidly proves at least that the average Christian, keen enough to read books about the faith, is far more deeply interested in the Sermon on the Mount and the parables of the Kingdom than he seems likely to be in justification by faith or the meaning of the phrase ' in Christ.'

The strength of the scholars' point of view lies in the fact that by the use of their touchstone they can define Christianity ; consequently their pronouncements, arbitrary as they may seem to be, are at least clear and intelligible. Widely-read books about the Jesus of the Gospels are sometimes impressionistic and cloudy ; their authors seem not to have thought out the difference between Christianity and modern idealism.   They assume that Jesus taught the universal fatherhood of God and the universal brotherhood of man, ignoring the fact that there is no actual evidence in the Gospels that He did either, however much we may wish He had.[1] On the other hand, scholars should more frankly recognize that there is, in the New Testament, another type of teaching, equally primitive and equally Christian, and

[1] See the present writer's *What did Jesus Teach ?* (pp. 25 ff.).

B

that it is impossible to fit everything, even in the most authentic Gospel sources, into the scheme of Pauline theology. Jesus is the teacher of a new way of life and the preacher of a Kingdom of obedience to the will of His Father as the law of life, as well as the bringer of salvation made possible by the grace of God mediated by the faith of man. The Acts of the Apostles tells us that the first name for the new religion was ' the way.' Ultimately the two points of view—Christianity as a law of life inspired by obedience to Jesus, and Christianity as a new power to live it depending on faith in Christ crucified and risen—lead us to the same place, for even a Barthian professor in my hearing defined faith as obedience. But we do an injustice both to the range of our religion and to the minds of those whom we would win to its allegiance, if we try to force them to enter either by one gate or the other. Most of us have come to see that ' Jesus or Paul,' like ' the Jesus of history ' or ' the Christ of experience,' is a misleading antithesis. Indeed, the older antithesis—' works versus faith '—has, I believe, outlived its usefulness ; this opposition too should be transcended by the idea of obedience inspired by love for the crucified and risen Lord, and sustained by His indwelling Spirit ; this binds together ' Take my yoke upon you and learn of Me,' and ' To me to live is Christ.'

There are and always have been three leading types of believer in the Church. The first and now the most numerous is represented by Peter and his fellow-apostles in the early days, and by the young people who have grown up in Christian homes in these. They are disciples, and have been drawn into Church membership by the idea of Jesus as the leader and master of all good living. The question which comes most naturally to them is not ' What must I do to be saved ? ' but ' What shall I do with my life ? ' The fact that Jesus chose such men to be His most intimate companions, and committed the founding of the Church to them in the first instance, that He never talked about their sin to them, but took them where they discovered for themselves what sinners they were, proves that this type now, as in the first days, is authentically Christian. If such disciples go on seeking to follow, they will sooner or later come to the Cross, and experience the new birth, without which not the best-intentioned of us can enter the Kingdom, but this may not be the beginning, but the *crown* of a long period of discipleship. Peter is ' the rock ' on which the Church is built, because the Church has been maintained from the beginning largely by men and women who find their way into the deeper realities of Christian experience gradually, and come to Calvary by way of Galilee.

A second quite distinct type is represented in the Gospels by the publicans and sinners, in the Pauline Churches by most of his converts from heathenism, and in the modern Church by many members of our mission churches. As the ' publicans ' in those early days were instantly at home with Jesus, so their modern representatives are to-day. Apparently Jesus said little to them about their sins any more than He did to Peter, for little needed to be said. The fact of their sin was hammered home upon them by words and looks, by the whole attitude of the respectable, every day of their lives. The message which wins them still is ' the wooing note,' the simple ' Come to Jesus.'

Paul represents a third class, very much less frequently to be found in the modern Church, but commoner now than in his day. Religion had always been the chief interest of his life, but it was religion considered in its ethical rather than its mystical or theological aspects. His experience of Christ made him a mystic, his sensitiveness to the needs of his converts, his pastoral heart, made him a theologian, but his starting point was an overwhelming sense of moral failure in himself and in the world about him. This is not characteristic of the Rabbinic religion in which he was brought up, and must have been native to his mind, for he certainly did not learn it from Gamaliel. He was at once an intensely earnest moralist and a religious genius of the first order, and it would be as foolish to estimate the quality of average Christian experience in the churches which he founded by Paul's language, as to imagine that Charles Wesley's hymns express the emotions of the average Methodist. No doubt we feel and are better for singing them, but neither their rapture nor their self-abasement is the natural language of our souls ; what wonderful people we should be, if it were so ! We may be sure there was an equally great gulf between Paul and the people he loved so well ; he was their father in Christ (1 Cor. iv, 15) and they admired him intensely, but I should imagine that his letters bewildered them as much as they have puzzled some later expositors. There are signs everywhere of the difficulty he found in making himself understood, and some of the mistakes expositors have made in interpreting him have been due to his habit of snatching at any illustration that came into his mind, never dreaming that scholars of a later day would busy themselves in building up elaborate theological systems from his *obiter dicta*.

Two things are worth mentioning in this connexion. He was a busy man, and, like other busy men, he probably never wrote a letter when he could possibly avoid doing so. His Epistles were generally written in moments spared from preaching, travelling, and tent-making ; he did not expect any one but the people for whom they were written to see them, and probably never mentioned to his travelling companions that he was writing an Epistle, unless its contents concerned them. It has been gravely doubted whether the Acts can have been written by a friend and companion of Paul like Luke, because its author shows so little knowledge of the Epistles. Surely this difficulty bespeaks a lack of imagination on the part of those who make much of it ; Paul would not think it necessary to give his friend a list of his letters or an account of their contents. I doubt whether he took himself as seriously as his commentators have done.

The second fact that should be borne in mind is that he dictated his letters, or rather the letters not written in prison, where no amanuensis would be available. If we want to test Paul's literary style, we must take Ephesians or Colossians as our standard. In prison he had leisure for long reflexion, and could elaborate. Usually, he only appended his name, except perhaps in Galatians, where he wrote the final sentences in his own ' large letters.' We may well imagine that he paced up and down the room, and that the copyist could scarcely keep pace with him; we may be sure that his mind and tongue would work at lightning speed. His love for tempting by-roads and the following-up of suddenly dawning ideas, his habit of parenthesis and the fertility of his imagination, all endear him to us, but it must never be forgotten that it is neither fair to Paul, nor to the faith which he lived to proclaim, to treat so mercurial a writer as though he weighed every word, and were writing a series of theological treatises.

Such men as Paul are little understood, but, all the more for that reason, are devotedly followed. They do not represent the age in which they live, and are more influential in later generations than in their own. Neither in his sense of sin nor in his rapturous exultation in redeeming love is Paul typical of the general mood of the Church then or now. What we feel vaguely and intermittently he felt at all times passionately, and his passion expresses depths within us, of which, it may be, we only become conscious when we are under the spell of great souls such as he was. But if he does not represent the mood of the Church or the normal course of Christian experience, he does interpret for us the soul which has kept the Church alive, something deeper than any surface-mood or ' spirit of the age.' When we listen to him the spirit within us finds its wings, and we understand ourselves. Paul is not the rock on which the Church is built ; he is rather the Moses who strikes the rock into life. And so he remains the supreme interpreter of life in Christ, in spite of the fact that his almost unique faculty of concentration upon religion—apparently to the exclusion of most other interests—makes it far easier to admire than to understand him. Yet fundamentally Paul's religion is utterly simple ; after his conversion, his one inspiring motive was a consuming passion for his Lord. Paul is not unrepresentative, because he thought more deeply than we, or because he did so much more than we can ever hope to do for the spread of the gospel, but because he loved far more intensely. We have many interests ; he had one : for us to live is many things ; for him to live was Christ.

CHAPTER I

SAUL OF TARSUS BEFORE CONVERSION

SUCH information as we possess concerning the early life of Saul of Tarsus comes from the Acts of the Apostles. In Acts xxii, 3 ff. Paul is made to say : ' I am a Jew, born in Tarsus of Cilicia, brought up in this city (Jerusalem) at the feet of Gamaliel, educated according to the rigour of our ancestral law.' Grave doubts have been expressed lately as to the accuracy of this statement, for Paul seems to mis-represent Rabbinic teaching, as we know it from other sources. It is true that these authorities are of later date, but Dr. Abrahams, perhaps the most sympathetic of all Jewish critics of the New Testament, declared that he could see no reason to believe that Rabbinic Judaism completely changed its tone in A.D. 70 when Jerusalem fell. The Rabbis did not teach, and never have taught, salvation by works, these authorities tell us, but salvation by the mercy of God answering the repentance of man. In this con-nexion a Rabbinic parable is quoted as typical. There was a ' prodigal son ' who in dire need sent a message to his father, telling him that he had not the means to come home, for the way was long. The father answered, ' Come as far as you can, my son, and I will come the rest of the way.' The angels, it was said, did not believe in the sincerity of Manasseh's repentance, and closed up all the avenues by which his prayer could reach the throne of God ; whereupon God opened a passage beneath the throne which they could not touch.

The question is : ' If Saul was trained by Gamaliel who,

admittedly, was one of the most liberal of the Rabbis, could he have so misunderstood and misrepresented the current teaching of the schools ? ' No one suggests that he consciously perverted the truth, but it is urged that he cannot have been trained in Jerusalem, certainly not at the feet of Gamaliel. There is, of course, no particular reason why the pupil should not be more fanatical than his teacher, but exaggerating a doctrine is one thing, altering its whole content is quite another.

This is a subject on which only an expert in Rabbinic theology can pronounce, but there are one or two considerations which may be mentioned here. If Paul misrepresents the Judaism of his day, the Gospels do so as well. Montefiore gives us a charming picture of Rabbinic teaching and practice ; as one reads his book, *Judaism and St. Paul*, or the contributions made by the Jewish writers to the Jewish-Christian symposium lately published by Hodder & Stoughton (*In Spirit and in Truth*), one gets the impression that the Rabbis were kindly teachers, who might indeed be called easy-going, for there is something almost smug about their healthy-mindedness. The fact remains that one of the best-authenticated sayings of Jesus runs : ' You bind heavy burdens upon men's backs,' addressed to these very Jewish teachers, and that the Gospel records are unanimous that the Rabbis and their pupils pursued Jesus with the most rancorous hostility. Is this also misrepresentation ? If Pharisaism was so tolerant, how did Jesus manage to get crucified at all, and how was it that Saul became a persecutor ? Jewish writers tell us that Jesus was crucified as a revolutionary by the Romans, not by Jewish bigotry. If so, Christian tradition must be false, for it is unanimous in its affirmation that, though the Romans may have carried out the sentence, the Jewish authorities were responsible, and Pharisees were in a majority in the Sanhedrin.

We must bear in mind that, by its own testimony, Pharisaism reformed itself after the destruction of the Jewish state which followed the revolt of Barcochba (A.D. 132), so that both Jesus and Paul had to meet a somewhat different Judaism from that represented by the Talmud and the *Sayings of the Jewish Fathers* from which our Jewish friends draw their examples of tolerance to confound us.   The fact is that the New Testament is our only *contemporary* witness to the condition of the Jewish Church in the years A.D. 30–70, for Josephus is too anxious to make the Jewish Sects respectable to the educated world by dressing them up as schools of philosophy to be reliable.   The Gospels tell us, moreover, that there were Liberal Rabbis—one of them plays a part in Mark xii, 28 ff.—while a very tolerant speech is put into the mouth of Gamaliel in Acts v, 34 ff., but it seems probable that such liberals as Hillel the carpenter and Gamaliel were in a small minority among their colleagues, and that the general drift of the party was increasing during between A.D. 30 and 70 towards a more bigoted nationalism in religion and politics.

This is precisely the burden of our Lord's attack upon the Pharisaic scribes ; they were misleading the people who were ' like sheep without a shepherd ' stampeding down the steep place into the abyss of futile rebellion against Rome, a rebellion which could only end in national suicide.   The scribes, with their unique influence in the synagogue, might have saved the situation ; instead of that they used the devotion of their followers to make them ' twice as much children of hell as they were themselves.'   Revolutionary sentiments they were too cautious to express were not discountenanced in their young admirers, and so they sent a whole generation to their deaths ; like hireling shepherds, they left their flocks at the mercy of the ' wolf ' of zealotry, which could only ' kill and destroy.' There is abundant evidence in the history of that generation to justify the attack made by Jesus upon the scribes, and the attractive description of Pharisaism after the final eclipse of the Jewish state does little to meet it.

We may infer that Saul of Tarsus was one of these fanatical young partisans of Judaism, but that his birth outside of the maelstrom of Palestinian politics and his own temperament, to which religion rather than any secular concern, even the liberty of his own country, must always have been the chief interest, concentrated his energy upon the defence of his people's faith rather than that of their freedom. One cannot but feel that, if Gamaliel's speech in Acts v, 34 ff. really represented Gamaliel's ideas, no ardent young pupil of his, however much he reverenced his teacher, could have been satisfied with such easy-going sentiments. After all, if the Rabbis taught salvation by repentance, was not Paul right in describing that as salvation by ' works of the law ' ? Whether held fanatically as by Saul of Tarsus, or tolerantly, as, apparently, by Hillel or Gamaliel, such a doctrine is deeply humanistic, and utterly contrary to the emphasis upon unmerited grace which became the burden of the Christian apostle Paul's preaching. One wonders, indeed, as one reads Montefiore, whether the truth is not that Paul has not so much misrepresented Rabbinic religion as exposed its real essence. The fundamental difference between Rabbinism and evangelical Christianity is that between a religion centred upon man's striving and a religion centred upon God's action.

Acts vi, 9 ff. suggests that Jews from the dispersion were active in opposition to Stephen, and the fact that ' Cilicia ' is mentioned as one of the provinces from which they came implies that Saul of Tarsus who appears in the narrative so soon afterwards (Acts vii, 58) was one of these assailants of the new ' way.'   In Palestine Jews were in the majority ; in the cities, their synagogues would be among the more imposing buildings in the town ; in the dispersion they were a despised minority.   Their influence upon certain types of Gentile was great, but it was subterranean, and they were intensely conscious of the pressure of paganism about them, and of their own real moral superiority.   The fact that Saul had been educated at a pagan university would only accentuate his self-consciousness ;   wherever he went, we may be sure that he was a marked man, for it was not in his nature to be anything but downright.   When he came to Jerusalem to have his education finished at the feet of Gamaliel, his opinions would be already formed, and perhaps the moderation of his teacher had little effect upon him.   Saul of Tarsus was, above everything, a moralist ; the description he gives of the tone of pagan society in Rom. i is that of a man who loathes vice with all the force of his soul.   Rabbis who had never stirred far away from home and synagogue, who had been cradled in the decencies of Judaism, might talk easily about doing your best and for everything else relying on the mercy of God, but Saul knew that the great world was rotten at heart (Rom. iii, 11 ff.) and honestly believed that its only hope lay in conversion to the religion which had made his home a refuge where the decencies, flouted in the streets and temples, could live and grow.   That religion he had from his earliest days been taught to associate with ' the law ' ; it was ' holy and righteous and altogether good ' (Rom. vii, 12), and all that he found at home and missed in the world outside was inseparable from it.

Did he know Jesus ? Neither the Acts nor his own Epistles give us any clear information on this question. At first reading, 2 Cor. v, 16, ' Even though we have known Christ after the flesh, yet now we know Him so no more,' might seem decisive, if it were not that Paul here writes ' Christ,' not ' Jesus,' and it was his custom always to use the name ' Jesus ' when he is speaking of the Jesus of history. Probably the meaning of this passage is : ' Even though we have known an earthly Messiah,' or ' thought of the Messiah in an earthly, secular, way.' ' Have not I seen Jesus our Lord ? ' (1 Cor. ix, 1) refers either to the vision on the Damascus road or to a subsequent trance-experience in the Temple (Acts xxii, 18). Dr. J. H. Moulton suggested that, inasmuch as the phrase translated ' God forbid ' is character-istic of Paul, the fact that it appears in Luke xx, 16, implies that Saul was the leader of the cry of protest with which the parable of the wicked husbandman was greeted. Perhaps this is too speculative to be taken seriously, but in any case it is unlikely that, if Saul was at that time a pupil of Gamaliel, he would not have been in Jerusalem at passover that year. If he was, he would surely have not been far away from the trial before Pilate and from Calvary. In this connexion we can only speak of probabilities, but it is more likely than not that he was an eyewitness of much that went on in Passion Week. ' I am Jesus whom thou persecutest ' (Acts xxvi, 15) suggests that Saul was persecuting Jesus Himself, not the Church only. The whole story of the conversion, as told three times over in the Acts, seems to imply that Saul already knew something of the Nazarene.

If he was present at the trial before Pilate and at the Cross, we may take it for granted that a young man so deeply religious as Saul of Tarsus was must have been impressed by the demeanour of the prisoner. Indeed, we may well imagine that the Pauline emphasis upon ' Christ and Him crucified,' owes its subconscious origin to that impression. But for the moment the Cross was, and could not but have been, what he calls (in 1 Cor. i, 23) a ' skandalon,' for the very idea that the Son of God could die a death on which God had set His curse was blasphemy.   There seemed to be no escaping the logic of facts ; if Jesus of Nazareth was allowed to die on a cross, He could not be God's Son, and, if He was not God's Son, He was a blasphemer.   Saul of Tarsus was a fundamentalist ; the ' Scripture cannot be broken ' (John x, 35) was a Rabbinic axiom, and the Scripture said ' Cursed is every one who hangs upon a tree ' (Deut. xxi, 23 ; Gal. iii, 13).   Unless Saul was to surrender the fundamental belief on which the whole structure of his life had been built, he could not become a follower of Jesus. No ; He had been a false teacher, notoriously friendly with disreputable people, and the fact that He was allowed to die on a cross, and acknowledge Himself forsaken at the end, made it only too clear that no God-fearing Jew could do anything but strive to extirpate this heresy.   Any favourable impression made by this blasphemer was a sin against God, to be atoned for only by signal service.   Jesus had said, according to the Fourth Gospel, ' any one who kills you will think he is doing God service ' (John xvi, 2) ; that might have been applied to Saul of Tarsus and sufficiently explains why he became a persecutor of the Church.

When he heard, some days later, that the Nazarene's followers were saying that He had risen from the dead, this would only be regarded as a culminating blasphemy.   But he does not seem to have been stung into action till Stephen became aggressive, and he was probably one of the young Jews of the dispersion who argued with him (Acts vi, 9 f.). Perhaps Saul had been away in Tarsus during the time that elapsed between the Crucifixion and the martyrdom of Stephen (probably six years), and when he returned was surprised to find the heresy still flourishing, indeed more dangerous than ever. F. C. Conybeare argued that, in Acts vii, 58, we should read ' they laid his (i.e. Stephen's) garments at the feet of a young man named Saul.' If he was right, Saul was already an official of the Sanhedrin ; this need not imply that he was a member of that body, for pupils of Rabbis were allowed to attend its meetings, though not to vote. All that Acts vii, 60 says is that ' Saul was in favour of his death ' ; it does not necessarily mean that he had a vote to cast against the accused.

The fact that Luke tells us that Stephen prayed for his murderers, as Jesus had done, and said ' Lord Jesus, receive my spirit,' as Jesus had said ' Father, into Thy hands I commend My spirit,' may suggest to us that his friend, Saul, had been impressed with the parallel. But, if so, for the time being it only increased his resentment. Why could not these people leave him alone ? He had been happy enough before they came into his life. But now he was growing uneasily conscious that these Nazarenes possessed a serenity which in these days was more than ever absent from Saul's own spirit. I think we may regard Rom. vii, 7 ff. as a real fragment of autobiography ; it is surely too specific and personal to be a mere dramatization of human experience. It was all very well for his teachers to tell him that he must not take his own moral failure too seriously, that God would pardon him. He could not be satisfied while there remained the increasing gap between theory and practice which he describes so realistically. To him it was like being tied up to a dead body which he had to drag about with him (vii, 24). He was beginning to wonder whether a religion of rules and obedience was not a mockery, whether he was not a hopeless slave fighting a battle the issue of which was decided before it had begun. Perhaps his teachers were just pretending, and had settled down to talk about obeying God's law, because talking about it was the only thing left to do.

If we have diagnosed not altogether incorrectly the war in Saul's soul, what would be his outward reaction to it ? He was the most loyal of men, a partisan by nature ; he would look upon the doubts which were tormenting him as a kind of treason. He would leave nothing for them to feed upon, would give himself no time to brood, would atone for his sinful thoughts by feverish activity. So he urged the Jewish authorities to action, and made the pace so hot that many Christians fled to Damascus, and of the leaders only the apostles were left in Jerusalem. It would seem that he did not think it worth his while to attack them ; they were quiet law-abiding members of the Jewish Church, and, if they were left alone, would soon forget their foolish notions, or drift away to Galilee again. As refugees from Jerusalem, these who had escaped to Damascus would still be regarded as under the control of the Sanhedrin. Saul set off to Damascus hoping that the authorities there would help him to discover the hiding-places of these Nazarenes. The fact that he was so busy betrays his state of mind ; he was becoming obsessed by this new movement, and could not leave it alone.

If our reconstruction of the working of Saul's mind before his conversion is anywhere near the truth, we cannot be surprised that when he was blinded by the light in the noonday sky and heard the voice of Jesus of Nazareth, when he realized that the Crucified who had died a cursed death had been raised to God's right hand, he took but little convincing; indeed he was more than half won already. Jesus, quoting a familiar Greek and Jewish proverb, told him that it was futile to resist any longer ; the harder he kicked, the further he drove the goad in. For three days he was blind ; it is likely that he bore the marks of the experience he had been through in his body as well as in his spirit to the end of his days, ' the marks of the Lord Jesus.' Led by his companions, he was taken to Damascus, where Ananias visited him and gave him his commission. There are three not quite harmonious accounts of his conversion in the Acts, but the general outline of the story is fairly clear. ' Have not I seen Jesus our Lord ? ' he wrote to the Corinthians later on (1 Cor. ix, 1). The rest of his life he spent in seeking to be not altogether unworthy to see the Lord again.

CHAPTER II

THE MISSIONARY

SAUL began, according to the Acts (ix, 20), to preach in the synagogues at once, the subject of his preaching being 'Jesus, the Son of God.' Neither Jews nor Christians would at first know what to make of this amazing change of front. But soon the Jews became violently hostile, and it was thought advisable for the new convert to leave the city for 'Arabia,' the country south of Damascus inhabited by the Nabatean Arabs. Aretas, whose daughter Herod Antipas had divorced in order to marry Herodias, was their sheik. It has been traditionally held that Saul went into retreat in 'Arabia,' but there is nothing to support this in the text either of the Acts or Galatians. It is more probable that he began his work among the Gentiles with these Arabs; it is not likely that many Jews were resident in this region. Aretas was hostile to them for personal reasons, and would resent the preaching of this Jewish superstition among his people. The consequence was that, three years later, he chased the young missionary out of the country back to Damascus, leaving his ethnarch, who was his responsible agent in dealing with Jews, to watch the city-gates to catch him if he tried to escape and trouble him again. While they watched the gates, Saul escaped by an opening in the wall away from the gates, through which he was let down in a basket (Acts ix, 23-25). The fact that in later days Paul includes this comparatively trivial incident in the catalogue of his sufferings shews how deep an impression this first humiliation made upon his mind (2 Cor.

C

xi, 32 f.).[1] Saul slipped away to Jerusalem to 'interview Cephas,' and stayed a fortnight with him.

Paul agrees with the account in Acts that the leaders of the Church in Jerusalem gave him a warm welcome, but others were not so friendly. One can scarcely blame them ; how could they be sure that he was not a spy collecting information against them by worming his way into their confidence ? But once more Saul found a friend, this time in Joseph Barnabas, who was able in a little while to disarm suspicions. But his old Jewish companions could not forgive him, and Saul was not the man to keep away from them or hide his convictions ; so for his own safety, and for the peace of the Church, he was sent away to Tarsus, where he disappears from sight for eleven years.

It was probably during this period that he 'suffered the loss of all things.' He would certainly be cut off by his people. He tells us (2 Cor. xi, 24) that 'five times' he received 'forty stripes but one.' This refers to official beatings in the synagogues, and, as it comes almost at the beginning of his catalogue, it seems probable that they were all administered during these years. At the end of the time he had been excommunicated and was thrown completely upon his own resources, without home or Church. Fortunately, like other sons of well-to-do Jewish families, he had been taught a trade, and kept himself by his tent-making. In later days, he reminded the elders of the Ephesian Church in his farewell address at Miletus, that he had maintained not only himself but also his fellow-missionaries by his labours ; he must have been an exceedingly good workman. However, his long years of frustration at

---

[1] Acts and 2 Corinthians do not agree in their description of this incident Of course, we must follow Paul's own account where it is available. I agree with Moffatt that 2 Cor. xi, 32 f. ought to follow v. 23.

last came to an end, again through the kindly offices of Barnabas. Barnabas had come to Antioch in Syria, where a partly Gentile Church had now been established by men who afterwards became Paul's close friends, and hearing that Saul was still at Tarsus, went to look him up. Saul's forlorn condition is suggested by the fact that he (Acts xi, 25 f.) had some difficulty in finding him. However, he managed to do so, and brought him to Antioch, where he soon became one of the leaders of the Church.

Apparent discrepancies between the Acts and Paul's own testimony (in the Epistle to the Galatians) as to what followed are perhaps best resolved by the suggestion[1] that Luke has told the story of Paul's second visit to Jerusalem twice over (Acts xi, 27 ff. ; xv, 1 ff.), quoting in xi, 27 ff. the tradition of the Church of Antioch, in xv, 1 ff. that of the Church at Jerusalem. The difficulty consists in the fact that in Galatians Paul only mentions *two* visits to Jerusalem before he wrote the Epistle, whereas Acts (ix, 26 ff.; xi, 27 ff. ; xv, 1 ff.) appears to mention *three* visits paid before the beginning of the Second Missionary Journey. This is important, because the question Paul is arguing in Galatians is that of his own authentic apostolic authority ; he did not receive it from man, but direct from ' a revelation of the Lord.' As capital was being made of the fact that he had stayed with Peter in Jerusalem shortly after his conversion, he is obliged to say exactly what happened when he did so. If he failed to mention one of his visits—it should be noticed that he asserts in the most solemn way that he is telling the whole truth (Gal. i, 20)—little imagination is needed to see how his opponents would have exploited such lack of frankness. Unless ' Galatia ' was evangelized

---

[1] See the present writer's *Commentary on the Acts of the Apostles* (S.C.M.), pp. 50 ff.

and the Epistle was written before the beginning of the Second Missionary Journey, we shall have either to charge Paul with only telling half the story, when, moreover, it was specially necessary to put all his cards on the table, or Luke with making a serious blunder.

Dr. Duncan, in his excellent *Commentary on Galatians*, lately published, thinks that we must adopt the first alternative. This means accepting what is called ' The South Galatian theory,' that is, the view that the Churches to which Paul wrote his Epistle were those of Pisidian Antioch, Iconium, Lystra and Derbe, founded on the First Journey, and finding room between the First Journey and the Council of Jerusalem for the Galatian Churches to show signs of succumbing to Judaistic propaganda, for Paul to write his letter—from Syrian Antioch—and for the letter to do its work so effectively that Paul is able to report progress in Jerusalem without a word about the trouble, and accept the compromise reached at the Council. Apart from the grave difficulty of believing that Galatians was written before the two Epistles to Thessalonica, chronological considerations still seem to preclude this attractive suggestion. There is only one alternative left, and that is, to suppose that, like many ancient historians, Luke has given us two accounts of the same visit. In the same way in the early chapters of the Acts, we have *two* accounts (one from Cæsarea, another from Jerusalem) of the experiment in voluntary communism (Acts ii, 44 ff. ; iv, 32 ff.), *two* accounts of an arrest and appearance before the Sanhedrin of the apostles (iv, 5 ff. ; v, 17 ff.) and probably *two* accounts of the way in which the great revival began (Acts ii, 1 ff. ; iii, 1 ff.). Antioch would naturally be chiefly interested in the collection which led to Saul's second visit to Jerusalem, Jerusalem itself in what took place when Saul and Barnabas arrived there. The fact that in Acts xi, 30, we read that the collection was sent ' to the elders ' does not necessarily mean that the apostles were not there, but that the apostles were not regarded as being concerned with financial matters (Acts vi, 2) which were administered by ' the elders ' (a larger body, representative of the local Church).

Acts xv certainly gives one the impression that Saul and Barnabas were sent for by the Church in Jerusalem to discuss relations between Jewish and Gentile Christians, Acts xi, 27 ff., that they were sent by the Church at Antioch with the collection, and for no other reason. But why should not advantage have been taken by the Church at Antioch of the fact that Barnabas and Saul were going up to Jerusalem with the collection to state their point of view on a question which (according to Acts xv, 1) was already agitating that Church ? We should notice that it is not said in that passage that the people who insisted that Gentiles could not be saved unless they were circumcised were believers ; it still seems to me far more likely that they were Jews masquerading as Christians, like the ' false brethren ' of Gal. ii, 4, who found their way into the Church without any right to be there, or the ' false apostles ' of 2 Cor. xi, 13. It is true that Acts xv, 5 says that ' some of the Pharisaic sect who had believed ' urged at Jerusalem that Gentile Christians should be bidden to obey the law of Moses, but it is one thing to plead this cause in their own Church, quite another to follow Paul from Church to Church and poison the minds of his people against him, and I still refuse to believe that the bitter enemies of Paul in Galatia were really members of the Church at Jerusalem at all.

As this controversy played so great a part in Paul's life and work as a missionary, it is important that we should comprehend the issues at stake. The matter was not so simple as some modern commentators would suggest, nor was the Jewish-Christian argument altogether unreasonable. We must remember that all parties were agreed that the Old Testament was the word of God ; it was the only Bible that the Church possessed, its text-book at once of Theology and Church polity. But if it was binding upon Christians, why not the whole Old Testament ? What business had any one to treat Isaiah as inspired, and ignore Leviticus ? We know how Paul dealt with the question in Galatians ; were his opponents very much to be blamed if they regarded his treatment of the sacred book as high-handed ? In any case, Jesus and His first disciples, they would argue, had been faithful members of the Jewish Church. It is true that Jesus was charged with breaking the Sabbath law, or encouraging others to break it, but, whatever His enemies said about Him, He never suggested to His followers that they should separate from Temple or synagogue, and, if He said, ' Go and make disciples of all the nations,' did He not mean ' disciples like yourselves ' who take the whole of the Old Testament as the word of God ? Perhaps Paul never quite settled this issue ; it is true that he used the Old Testament itself—most ingeniously—to prove that parts of the sacred book were for all Christians, while other parts were only meant for the Jews, but it was left for the author to the Hebrews to work out a philosophy of revelation, a task which Paul was too busy with practical problems to attempt. I am not suggesting that the Jewish-Christians were right, merely pointing out that, on Paul's own premises, there was more to be said for them than is generally allowed. As J. R. Mozley said, from the early Christian point of view (accepted by Paul), there had been only one dispensation from the Creation, and that was the dispensation of the gospel.

Arguing from this premise, it was difficult to see why any part of the Old Testament should be relegated to a secondary place in Christian theory and practice. Furthermore, many of these Gentile converts came into the Church from pagan surroundings ; might they not carry some of their heathen habits with them and seriously lower its tone ? This was a real danger, as Paul's letters abundantly show ; ought they not, then, to have some kind of moral code, recommended to them as the rule of the Church ? The 'Sibylline Oracles'[1] prove that in the first century A.D. some Jews were willing to receive Gentile converts into Judaism by baptism *without circumcision*, if they accepted the true God, and abjured idolatry, murder, fornication and sodomy. The 'Western' text of Acts xv, 20, 29, suggests that something on these lines was accepted by the 'Council of Jerusalem,' 'that they should abstain from abominations of idols and from fornication and blood' (interpreted as 'the taking of life ') ; some, but not all, 'Western' authorities add a negative version of the 'golden rule,' which Jesus had said summed up, 'the law and the prophets.' I am convinced that in this case the 'Western' text is right, for it is inconceivable that, even at this early stage in his career, Paul could have accepted a food law (the 'things strangled' of the Received Text) as binding upon *Gentile* Christians. The word translated 'things strangled' was added because, as a matter of fact, in the second century many Christians (in North Africa and Gaul) did observe such a food law ; it is really a misinterpretation of 'blood' in the original. The point here is that there was a case for imposing some elementary moral regulations on Gentile converts, in having, in other

---

[1] The Jews in the first century A.D. began to propagate their faith partly by attributing certain 'oracles' of Judaistic origin and tendency to the heathen prophetess, 'the Sibyl,'

words, rules of membership, and that Paul would not have objected to this.

But behind all this there was another even more vital question. How were Jewish and Gentile Christians to live together in the Church? Were the Jews to become, to all intents and purposes, Gentiles by breaking their own food-law—which was an integral part of their religion—or were Gentiles to become Jews? On this issue three positions were possible. Peter had been induced by his vision at Joppa to take the bold line and eat with Gentiles, thus once and for all separating himself from Judaism. This was a great step forward, and it is not surprising that his fellow Jewish Christians demanded an explanation of his action in going to the house of Cornelius and eating Gentile food. There is no evidence that this had ever been done before, even by Jesus; Peter was the pioneer in this, as in some other respects; the fact that he 'withdrew himself' later should not disqualify him from receiving the honour that is his due. We shall deal with the difference of opinion between Peter and Paul later; meanwhile we should notice that Paul charges him and Barnabas with inconsistency, not with being a reactionary. James, the brother of the Lord, was not prepared to take so radical a step, but, according to Luke—and I see no reason for distrusting his statement— did not wish to make the Gentiles comply with his ideas; he visualized two separate Churches side by side, one Jewish and the other Gentile. Then there was the third position maintained by some converted Pharisees, that the Gentile converts should be circumcised, and become Jews when they became Christians.

It may be argued, in favour of the early date here sug-gested for the Council, that the comparatively passive part taken by Saul is much more intelligible if it took place before rather than after the First Missionary Journey. But the objection may still be raised that Paul himself tells us that Titus was with him on his second visit to Jerusalem, and it has generally been assumed that Titus' association with Paul only began subsequently. But this is pure assumption, for the New Testament itself gives us no information as to when and where Paul and Titus first met. If, as has been reasonably conjectured from Luke's silence about Titus, he was Luke's own brother—translating ' the brother ' of 2 Cor. viii, 18 as ' his ' (i.e. ' Titus' ') brother—there is nothing to make the suggestion that they met at Antioch untenable, for Luke is already connected in Church tradition and by the ' Western ' text of Acts xi, 27 with Antioch. Whether Titus was circumcised or not is not clear from Paul's cryptic statement in Gal. ii, 3. If we say ' not even Titus . . . was compelled to be circumcised,' we might infer that Titus *was* circumcised, but not because of any pressure put upon him by Paul, rather at his own request. On the other hand, if emphasis is laid on the word ' circumcised,' the suggestion seems to be that he was not. Personally, I am inclined to think that he was, but not at Paul's desire. The question as to the exact meaning of the whole passage will come up in a later chapter.

On their return from the Council, Barnabas and Saul were commissioned by the Church at Antioch to undertake a mission-tour. They take with them John Mark, who had come to Antioch from Jerusalem with Barnabas his cousin. In Cyprus, where the mission began, Saul made a deep impression on the governor of the island, Sergius Paulus, largely because of his victory over a professional magician, whose name was Elymas (or perhaps ' Hetoimas '). Here for the first time Luke mentions (Acts xiii, 9), in a tantalizingly casual way, the name by which Saul was henceforth to be

known ('Paul')—'Saul who, by the way, was also Paul.'
I cannot believe that Saul could have called himself after
his first important convert; it is much more likely that this
was his name taken in baptism. Various interpretations
have been offered. One is that it was a nickname applied
to himself by Saul with a kind of playful humility. He
was 'of unimpressive personality' (2 Cor. x, 10) and small
stature, and 'paulus' means 'little,' or, perhaps, he was
alluding to the fact that he felt himself to be 'less than the
least of all saints' (Eph. iii, 8), that 'abortion of an apostle'
(1 Cor. xv, 8). Another suggestion is that it comes from a
Semitic root meaning 'chosen.' There is, of course, the possi-
bility that, like Mark, he had a Roman as well as a Hebrew
name, and that 'Paul' was simply his Roman name, conferred
upon him as a 'free-born' (Acts xxii, 28) citizen of Rome.

From Cyprus the party went across the water to Asia
Minor. There John Mark left them, and returned to
Jerusalem. It has been gratuitously assumed that his
defection was due to cowardice. It is more likely that
he was annoyed at the fact that his cousin Barnabas was
being more and more completely overshadowed by Paul;
Luke hints that this was the case, for, whereas in Acts xiii, 7,
the order is still 'Barnabas and Saul,' in xiii, 13, we have already
'those about Paul,' and at this point Mark abruptly departs.
(Notice the order Paul and Barnabas in xiii, 50.) It is
quite likely that at this stage in his career Paul was, like
John Wesley in his younger days, a somewhat overbearing
personality. At Pisidian Antioch he holds the floor, and
we have his first reported address. It is singularly like
Peter's speech at Pentecost, the only hint of 'Pauline'
doctrine coming at xiii, 38 f. In xiii, 50, we read how the
missionaries had their first taste of an experience which was
repeated at their next stopping-place, Iconium. They were

driven from the town by Jewish opposition, in which at Iconium the Gentiles joined.

At Lystra their adventures were still more exciting. In consequence of Paul's healing of a lame man—his first exploit of this kind of which we are told—Paul and Barnabas are on the point of being worshipped as Hermes and Zeus respectively, when they realize what is happening, and succeed with difficulty in avoiding this embarrassing compliment. ' Paul,' Luke tells us, was identified with Hermes, the most vivacious of the gods, ' because he did the talking.' However, their popularity was short-lived, for, with the arrival of Jews from Iconium, the crowd is persuaded to set upon Paul—it is interesting to observe that Barnabas is not involved—and he is stoned, and left for dead by the roadside. Before this happens he makes a second speech, which is a good example of his early missionary preaching (cf. 1 Thess. i, 9 f.). He may have alluded to this terrible experience in Gal. vi, 17. When the crowds have exhausted their fury, he was assisted to his feet by his friends, and arrived at Derbe, where he secured the lifelong loyalty of Timothy, and by and by was able to return on his tracks to the coast, and sail to Syrian Antioch. The question whether the Churches founded on this tour were the 'Galatians' to which, later on, Paul addressed the Epistle, will be dealt with in a later chapter.

Soon after his return to the home-base, Paul had two unpleasant experiences. Peter came to Antioch, and at first followed his custom, now habitual with him, of eating with his Gentile fellow-believers. However, when friends of James, the Lord's brother, who were not prepared to do so, arrived, he and Barnabas withdrew and with their friends from Jerusalem started a separate table. Paul was far-sighted enough to see that this action made a rift in the

Church, and ' withstood Peter to his face, because he was
clearly in the wrong.' We can see that he was right,
though Peter might, if he had thought it worth his while,
have put up a strong case in his own defence. He might
have argued that he had made his position perfectly clear,
and that, on the principle of ' being all things to all men,'
which Paul himself adopted later on (1 Cor. ix, 22), he
had a perfect right, having made a sacrifice of his predilections already and having suffered for it, to avoid a
needless break with older friends, and keep his foot in both
camps. Paul would have none of these specious arguments,
for he saw that, if there was a high and a low table, so to
speak, Gentile Christians would be eager, so great was the
prestige of Peter, to qualify for the high table, and so the
division in the Church would be perpetuated. I have no
doubt that Paul was right ; but I have an uneasy feeling
as I read Gal. ii, 14 ff. that it would have been more
gracious to have taken Peter to task privately, and that the
latter comes well out of this difference of opinion, in so far
as he refrained from putting his side of the case before the
Church ; apparently he neither cared to defend himself,
nor to entrust his defence to any of his friends, though he
must have known that Paul was likely to tell the story
from his own point of view later on, as indeed he did.

At the beginning of the Second Missionary Journey Paul
and Barnabas parted company, nominally over the question
of taking Mark with them again. I suspect that the difference went deeper than that, and that Barnabas resented the
line his colleague and friend had taken in his attack on
Peter. Luke frankly tells us that there was a ' sharp
quarrel ' between the two, and they very sensibly parted ;
Barnabas took Mark with him to Cyprus, and Paul took
Silas as his colleague. Silas, whose full name was Silvanus

(1 Peter v, 12; cf. 2 Cor. i, 19; 1 Thess. i, 1; 2 Thess. i, 1), had come with Paul and Barnabas from Jerusalem after the Council, and was apparently, like Paul, a Roman citizen (Acts xvi, 37). It was useful for Paul to have a companion with the same privileges as he himself enjoyed. Silas, it may be mentioned, drops out of Luke's narrative with strange suddenness, for we are not told why he and Paul parted company at Corinth.

Paul and Silas visited the Churches evangelized on the first journey, but in reverse order, beginning with Derbe; they crossed the Taurus and approached the cities of the Galatian plateau from the other end. At Derbe they picked up Timothy; Luke says rather strangely that Paul 'took and circumcised him, because of the Jews in those parts, for all knew that his father was a Greek' (Acts xvi, 3); we should have expected 'that his mother was a Jewess.' Paul's reason was, apparently, that Jews regarded children of a Gentile father and a Jewish mother as illegitimate; he is still anxious to conciliate Jewish opinion. The missionaries are now on the high-road to Ephesus, the capital of Asia and the third city in the Roman world. But a series of remarkable interventions prevented them reaching their objective. First, 'the Holy Spirit' forbade them to preach in Asia, and they were checked at the boundary of the province. Silas, we know, was a 'prophet' (Acts xv, 22), and perhaps the intimation came to him, for a 'prophet' in the New Testament sense of the word was one who was specially susceptible to such revelations of the divine purpose (cf. Acts xi, 27, where Agabus makes an inspired suggestion). I think it is quite likely, however, that the intimation came to Paul himself; it became a principle with him not to 'build on another man's foundation' (Rom. xv, 20); perhaps there was a Church already in

Ephesus, for, when he finally arrived there, he 'found' some disciples (Acts xix, 2), Christians already, though not very advanced Christians. Paul's refusal to visit places where another man was at work was due, we may suppose, to his fear of setting up divided loyalties. We may wonder who this other man was ; I should guess ' John the elder,' inasmuch as the Church at Ephesus cherished a ' Johannine ' tradition ; in any case, it does not seem likely that John was still there when Paul arrived a year or two later, for he would scarcely have allowed converts to enter the Church who had never heard of the Holy Spirit (Acts xix, 2). But this is a difficult question, on which it would be foolish to dogmatize.

There was nothing left for it but to follow the boundary of the province northward till they came to Mysia. At that point the road to the thickly-populated province of Bithynia led away to the north-east, and Paul was at first inclined to follow it, but here there was a more serious interposition ; ' the spirit of Jesus,' says Luke, ' would not allow them to do so ' (Acts xvi, 7). This can mean nothing else than that Jesus Himself intervened in Paul's private devotions ; all alternatives to the evangelization of Europe are one by one being made impossible. So they took the other (Western) road which led to Troas, which was to play an eventful part in Paul's history. There apparently he was visited by his old friend Luke, who may have had connexions with Macedonia, and suggested a mission there. In his sleep that night Paul saw the vision of the ' man from Macedonia ' ; this finally convinced him that he must take the plunge, without waiting for instructions from Antioch. The fact that Paul took so much persuading, I imagine, was due to the nature of his instructions from headquarters ; he was to go on with the evangelization of Asia Minor begun on the

First Journey. Later on Peter, or one of Peter's disciples, wrote a circular letter to the Churches of Bithynia and Pontus and (? North) Galatia (1 Peter i, 1) ; did Peter take up the work that Paul was not able to finish ? The fact that the First Epistle of Peter was addressed precisely to the parts of Asia Minor where Paul had not founded Churches at least suggests that it was believed that Peter had some connexion with them. The more I think of it, the more convinced I feel that the great missionary Church at Antioch set itself to cover the whole of Asia Minor.

Paul, Silas, Timothy and Luke crossed the water, and made their first prolonged halt at Philippi ; it was not the capital of the province, as a cursory reading of Acts xvi, 12, might suggest ; perhaps we should accept the reading ' a city of the first district of Macedonia,' for Macedonia had been divided into four districts in 167 B.C. Here there was apparently no synagogue, but only a Jewish place of prayer—in the open-air by the river Gangites. The mission in Europe had a quiet beginning, for Paul and his colleagues simply talked to the devout women who attended the Jewish services ; probably they were Gentiles, though we cannot be certain of this. One of them became Paul's first convert in Europe ; it is curious that Paul, whose letters show so little appreciation of women, should have had so much influence with them. The story of Paul's adventures at Philippi is too familiar to need repetition. It is character-istic of him that he should let the magistrates beat two Roman citizens, and then inform them of what they had done in the morning. The Church at Philippi, among the first members of which were a well-to-do business woman, a clairvoyant slave-girl who told fortunes, and the town gaoler with his family, was perhaps the best-loved and the most generous of his Churches.

When the missionaries went on to Thessalonica, they were again immediately successful. The fact that in Phil. iv, 16, Paul says that ' twice during his stay in Thessalonica the Philippians had sent a contribution to his support,' shows that he must have spent more than the three weeks of Acts xvii, 2, there. Again Paul succeeded in winning the adherence of women of good social standing, but the mission, so prosperously begun, met with an unfortunate interruption. The Jews, jealous of Paul's success, were soon busy making trouble, and bribed low-class agitators to create a disturbance. The result was that a mob appeared at Jason's house, where the missionaries were staying. Unhappily they were not to be found, and Jason was dragged before the magistrates, who extracted from him a promise that his guests should abandon their work in Thessaly. Jason gave his word of honour, and Paul and Silas were compelled to leave Thessalonica, leaving behind them in the minds of those not acquainted with the facts the impression that they had run away.

At Beroea, their next stopping-place, they were well received, and were just settling down when again the Jews came along. Apparently the jurisdiction of the officials at Thessalonica extended throughout the sub-province of Thessaly ; the ' Western ' text has in xvii, 15 : ' and he passed by Thessaly, for he was prevented from speaking the word to them.' Silas and Timothy, however, were left behind in Beroea, and Paul went on alone to Athens. It would seem that the ban upon preaching in Thessalonica did not include Timothy, for 1 Thess. iii, 2, tells us that Timothy was sent back there.

1 Thess. iii, 1, suggests that Paul was lonely and depressed when he waited in Athens for the return of his assistant-preachers ; masterful as he was and sometimes in those

early days a little difficult to work with, it is interesting to
observe that he never founded a Church *alone*, and that he
depended more than we should have expected on com-
panionship. However, the sight of the city's amazing
variety of religions proved too much for him, and it is
not very long before he is at work again. As many men
have done since, he tries to adapt himself to an educated
audience, including in his address before the Areopagus
at least two learned quotations. Aratus, one of the poets
quoted, came from Tarsus, so perhaps we should render
Acts xvii, 28, ' *our* local poets ' ; Paul was evidently proud
of his home city and its culture (cf. Acts xxi, 39). The other
quotation comes from a hymn to Zeus attributed to Epimenides, a mythical son of Zeus, attacking the Cretans
who declared that Zeus was dead, and showed his tomb :
the complete quotation runs :

They made a tomb for thee, most renowned, most great one
The Cretans, always liars, evil beasts, mere idle bellies
But thou dost not die, but standest alive for ever,
For in thee we live and move and have our being (cf. Tit. 1, 12).

Epimenides is said to have been called in by the Athenians
to the city after an outbreak of plague, and to have set up
altars to the gods, including the unknown (i.e. unnamed)
local deities of the Acropolis. No one has ever in ancient
or modern times discovered an altar to ' the unknown god '
at Athens ; we must infer that Paul had seen this altar to
' unknown gods.' He was at first listened to with curiosity,
but when he began to speak of ' Resurrection ' his audience
became restive ; they understood the idea of immortality,
—for had they not their own Eleusinian mysteries ?—but
professed to imagine that ' Anastasis ' (Resurrection) was
some strange female deity. Paul had some slight success ;

D

two converts—a man and a woman—are mentioned, but no Church was founded, and he tells us that ' the household of Stephanas ' (1 Cor. xvi, 15) were his ' first converts in Achaia ' ; perhaps he means simply that they were his first family to join the Church in the province. But we may suspect that his Athenian converts fell away. The epithet ' cock sparrow ' given him at Athens (Acts xvii, 18) is interesting as another suggestion of Paul's smallness of stature as well as of his vivacity.

Still alone, Paul went on to Corinth, where after a time Silas and Timothy joined him. There he made lasting friends of Aquila and Priscilla, who had come from Rome, and were, like himself, tentmakers. Partly from his own observation, partly perhaps from the information about Corinth given him by his new friends, he decides to change his plan of campaign, and henceforth to ' know nothing '— at least in Corinth—' except Jesus Christ and Him crucified.' In a later chapter we shall discuss the development of his missionary message ; it is not unlikely that his unsatis-factory experiences at Thessalonica and at Athens were a deciding factor in his resolve to leave the sphere of natural for that of revealed theology. As was his habitual practice, he began work at the synagogue, and was quickly successful. When Silas and Timothy arrived, Paul went at it harder than ever, and the consequence soon was that the meeting was divided, and a rival conventicle set up next door. Apparently Aquila and his wife carried on in the original meeting. Paul stayed in Corinth for eighteen months. The Church there was perhaps the largest and wealthiest of all his flocks ; it was his most spectacular success, but caused him almost endless trouble. He wrote no fewer than four letters to and received at least one letter from Corinth. Two incidents made the long sojourn there memorable. One was a vision, in which Paul was encouraged by the Lord Himself to go on with his work, the other was another riot engineered by the Jews, who dragged Paul before the judgement-seat of Gallio, the newly-arrived proconsul. In a lordly way Gallio refused to listen to their complaints, and even ignored the scuffle which followed. Whether Sosthenes, the ruler of the synagogue, was a convert of Paul's, and was identical with the Sosthenes of 1 Cor. i, 1, we do not know. The Received Text does not tell us who beat him ; the 'Western' text says it was the Greeks, who took the opportunity of Gallio's evident dislike of Jews to work off old scores ; perhaps both sides turned on the unlucky man.

At the end of the eighteen months Paul decided to make his long-deferred visit to Ephesus, and after taking a Nazirite vow—he must have been intending to go on to Jerusalem, for the vow had to be fulfilled there—he set sail with Priscilla and Aquila. It will be observed that the order in which this famous pair is named has changed ; it is easy to see that the wife was the predominant partner. They had been in Rome before they came to Corinth; perhaps the information they gave him about Christian meetings in the Capital of the Empire first suggested the idea that from Jerusalem he would go to Rome (Rom. xv, 25 ff.). He did not stay long at Ephesus, however, but soon—after one or two discussions with the Jews at the synagogue— set off again and landed at Caesarea.

At this point the story in the Acts becomes vague and hurried ; indeed, the so-called 'Third Missionary Journey' begins at a comma (xviii, 23). Did Paul go up to Jerusalem ? If he did, would the visit have been slurred over in the words 'he went up and saluted the Church' ? Does the word 'up' mean 'up to Jerusalem' or merely 'up from the

port of Caesarea to the town '? It is difficult to imagine
why Paul should travel to Palestine at all, unless he intended
to go to Jerusalem, but, if he did, why is Luke so mysterious
about it ? The Lake-Cadbury commentary suggests that he
only landed in Caesarea instead of Antioch, because with
certain winds it is easier to land there ; ' if, as often happens,
the winds are east of north, it is difficult for boats coming
from Ephesus to point as high as Antioch.' But the ' vow '
taken at Cenchreae and the fact that the ' Western ' text
says in so many words that Paul intended to go to Jerusalem
(xviii, 21) lead me to infer that he changed his mind at
Caesarea ; we can only wonder why.

From Caesarea Paul went on to Antioch, and then set off
to Ephesus again, visiting the Galatian Churches on the
way. His three years at Ephesus proved to be the turning
point in his career. For some reason Luke is decidedly
secretive about them, only reporting two incidents, and
mentioning that during part of the time Paul was in the habit
of holding meetings in the lecture-hall of a professional
lecturer named Tyrannus, the ' Western ' text says from 11
a.m. to 4 p.m. ' There would be more people asleep in
Ephesus at 1 p.m. than at 1 a.m.' says the Lake-Cadbury
commentary. Paul was evidently living a strenuous life ;
Tyrannus would lecture in the evenings, and Paul hired
the hall during the hot hours, working at his trade before
11 and after 4. In Acts xx, 34, Paul gives us the interesting
information that he supplied not only his own needs, but
those of his companions, by his labours.

The two stories that Luke tells us are both interesting.
Paul found some ' disciples ' at Ephesus who had never
heard of the Holy Spirit, and had only been ' baptized into
John's baptism.' This reminds us of Apollos, who,
according to Acts xviii, 25, when he first came to Ephesus,

'taught accurately the things concerning Jesus,' but only
understood the baptism of John, until Priscilla and Aquila,
in the order named, succeeded in converting the preacher
to a more complete Christianity. We should have inferred
that both Apollos and the disciples at Ephesus belonged
to the John the Baptist Church which was an active rival
both to orthodox Judaism and Christianity at this time,
if the former had not ' known accurately . . . about Jesus '
and the latter had not been called ' disciples.' We are
forced, I think, to conclude that in non-Pauline Churches,
such as Ephesus and Alexandria, from which Apollos
came, and in which he had been ' instructed in the way of the
Lord,' a non-Pentecostal Christianity was being preached,
and that Paul and Priscilla are both combating it.

The other story—that of the riot at Ephesus—is too
realistic to need much comment. There are two specially
illuminating points in the story ; one is the attempt of the
Jew Alexander to represent the Jewish interest, and his
shouting down by the crowd. If he is identical with
' Alexander the coppersmith ' of 2 Tim. iv, 14—this is a
genuine Pauline fragment—he was able afterwards to make
himself objectionable, but at the moment his attempt to
speak might have turned the riot into an anti-Jewish po-
grom but for the intervention of the town clerk. The
other point is What was the proconsul doing all the time
and why did the town clerk refer to the office of proconsul in
so vague a way ? 'There are such things as proconsuls ' he
says (Acts xix, 38). There should have been *one* proconsul at
Ephesus ; we cannot help wondering whether this riot
did not take place after the murder of Junius Silanus, the
proconsul, at the instigation of Agrippina, who sent two
men nominally to look after her estates in Ephesus, really
to assassinate Silanus, whom she suspected of plotting

to supplant her son Nero on the throne of the empire. For the whole question of Paul's three years' ministry in Ephesus, and the reasons for thinking that Luke's reticence is deliberate, I must refer readers to *St. Paul's Ephesian Ministry* by Dr. G. S. Duncan (Hodder & Stoughton).

Luke gives one the impression that the ministry in Ephesus was triumphantly successful. Paul became for a while an almost legendary figure; the very workman's aprons which he wore, the cloth with which he wiped the perspiration from his brow, were reported to have healing virtues, and were gathered up and treasured. Ephesus was quite different from Corinth, which boasted at once of its night-life and its culture. Corinth belonged to the West, Ephesus to the East. In Rev. ii, 2, and Acts xix, 13, it is hinted that religious charlatans of all kinds abounded there, and in Acts xix, 19, we hear of a colossal bonfire of expensive magical books. The Church was, we are told in the Apocalypse, lacking in stability; nowhere was Paul idolized more (see Acts xx, 37 f.), nowhere apparently forgotten so quickly. But Ephesus is immortal, because it gave to the Church the Fourth Gospel, and also because Paul's experiences of dazzling success followed by suffering and humiliation, unique even in his career, left him, if not a more heroic—he could not be that—certainly a gentler man, not a greater missionary, at least a greater saint, and produced his greatest Epistles.

There are many hints, in letters written during those years, that the half of Paul's sufferings at Ephesus has never been told. In 1 Cor. iv, 9, he says : 'God exposed us apostles as men last in a triumphal procession, doomed to die ; we became a spectacle to the universe, to angels and to men alike,' and in iv, 13 ; 'we are like the sweepings of the world's streets, everybody's whipping-boys ; so it has ever

been, and so it is just now.' Again in the same Epistle
(xv, 32) : ' If I had, as, humanly speaking, I might well have
done, actually fought with wild-beasts '—that is, ' If I had
been exposed to the wild-beasts in the arena '—'at Ephesus.'
There are many ways of interpreting this passage ; there is
certainly nothing in the story of the riot of Ephesus in Acts
xix, 21 ff., to justify such language. It is by no means
out of the question that the book called ' The Acts of Paul '
(A.D. 100) preserves a true tradition in this respect at least,
that Paul came very near to being thrown to the beasts.
Again, in Rom. xvi, 3 ff. Paul tells his readers that Priscilla
and Aquila ' laid down their necks ' for him ; it is not surprising perhaps that Luke should put the lady before her
husband ; it is amazing that Paul should do so, for he was
no feminist. The reference must be to a time later than
that at which 1 Cor. xvi, 13, was written, for in that passage
this couple is referred to in a comparatively cool way, the
husband's name coming first. The risking of their lives
on Paul's behalf cannot then have happened in the same
crisis as that referred to in 1 Cor. xv, 32. Last of all, in 2
Cor. i, 8 f., Paul tells us that he ' had despaired of life,'
that ' he had the answer of death in himself ' ; this might, of
course, refer to serious illness, and there are indeed many
signs of ill-health in the Corinthian letters, but there are
also suggestions in the same passage of external danger and
trouble. Dr. Duncan thinks that Paul was imprisoned
three times during this period, twice at Ephesus, and once
perhaps at Laodicea. We do not know what service
Priscilla and her husband were able to render Paul, but it
must have amounted to a real saving of his life at extreme
risk to themselves ; Paul says (Rom. xvi, 3 f.) ' Whom not
only I, but all the Churches of the Gentiles, have reason to
thank.' We may conjecture, perhaps, that a period of

anarchy followed the assassination of Silanus, that Paul and perhaps Priscilla, who may have been a freed woman of the famous ' Gens Prisca ' at Rome, had been under the protection of Silanus. After his murder, Paul's Roman citizenship would not protect him, for the unscrupulous ruffians who usurped the office of proconsul would not hesitate to make away with any one who had been associated with Silanus. Priscilla was able, at great personal risk, to save Paul's life ; she was quite clearly a lady of influence and strong character. Luke passed over the whole affair in silence because Paul was to be tried before Nero, and it would not help his case if it were known that he had been under the protection of Nero's murdered rival. I am convinced that all the Epistles of the imprisonment (Ephesians, Colossians, Philippians, Philemon) as well as the four Corinthian Epistles, were written during this period. With the change in Paul's character which took place then I hope to deal in a later chapter.

At the end of the three years, according to Acts xx, 1 ff., Paul set off by himself for a tour through Macedonia to Corinth, where he spent three months. He was on the point of setting sail for Syria again, with the intention of paying his long-expected visit to Jerusalem, when he heard of a Jewish plot against him, and decided to change his plans. So he retraced his steps through Macedonia, and, crossing the water again, met his friends at Troas. Luke had been in Paul's company, if Duncan is right, in Ephesus (Col. iv, 14 ; Philem. 24), and he now rejoins him. The whole party took the Lord's Supper together, and Paul went on talking all night, his address being interrupted by the fall of sleepy Eutychus from a window-sill into the street. But the fall was not fatal, and Paul set off with Luke and the others next morning. Paul was apparently not a very good sailor, and preferred to walk along the coast road to Assos; in the open water between Troas and Assos the north-east wind prevails for five days out of seven, and 'those only accustomed to steam-ships have no idea of the misery a north-east wind in the Mediterranean can cause.'

His friends picked him up at Assos, and they went on to Miletus together; there Paul calls the elders of the Church at Ephesus, and delivers to them a farewell address, which he had prepared on his long solitary walk along the coast. He is aware that his career as an itinerant missionary is nearly over. Twice over he had been foiled, when he had planned to go to Jerusalem; that can only mean one thing; his Jewish opponents are bent on his murder. The speech at Miletus is the only speech delivered to a Christian community preserved in the Acts, and it has evidently been taken down word by word. It is very moving; because of all that he has been through, any opposition to him within the Churches is silenced; he has won that battle. Now he is going to his death; he knows it, and so do they, and his listeners hang upon his words. They of all people in the world know best what he has been through, and are full of foreboding of what is to come for him, and for them, when he is gone. There are none of Paul's glancing asides, no tangled sentences; he has prepared his address with unusual care. The speech can only be compared with his last dying testament to Timothy (2 Tim. iv, 6 ff.). At the end of the speech there follows a great outburst of emotion. No doubt they had all had their differences with him, but now they realize all that this strangely self-contained and quiet little man means to them, and Paul at last wins his tribute of affection from his people.

Before we hasten to the climax of Paul's missionary

career, we must ask why, like his Master before him, he threw himself upon Jerusalem and his fate, against the entreaties of his friends and the warnings of inspired mediums like Agabus ? Arrest would certainly mean death sooner or later ; I cannot believe that Paul had many illusions as to the result of his appeal to Caesar. He believed (Rom. xiii, 3 ff.) in the soundness of Roman justice ; perhaps it would be truer to say that he *had* believed in it until it failed him in Ephesus. But how could any one who had seen the results of Silanus's assassination expect fair treatment from Nero, whose mother had been responsible for that outrage ? That is one of the reasons why I feel sure that Rom. xiii, 1 ff. must date from his stay in Corinth, i.e. before the Ephesian crisis. Rom. xvi, 3 f. must have been written *after* that crisis, and so does not belong to the main body of the Epistle. No ; he will make a fight for it, and carry his case, and with it the cause of Christianity, to the highest tribunal of the empire, but he knows what the result will be ; he was no blind optimist.

If we are to understand why Paul insisted on going to Jerusalem, we must go back to the question of the relation of Jews and Gentiles in the Church discussed earlier in this chapter. The chief pastoral concern of the first part of Paul's missionary career had been the defence of his Gentile converts against Jewish-Christian suspicions ; the predominant interest of his later years became reconciliation between the two parties, in other words, Christian unity. This greatest of all causes became a passion with him, and turned him into a money-raiser, a vocation for which he had considerable aptitude—witness the remarkably clever collection-appeal in 2 Cor. viii and ix—but little inclination. He set to work to organize a collection from his Gentile Churches for the benefit of the Churches of Judaea, which had fallen on evil days. That he had from the beginning a warm admiration for those Churches is clear from 1 Thess. ii, 14, one of the reasons for that admiration being, it may be, the fact that they had made the experiment of voluntary communism, to which his own Churches had never aspired. If he could raise a respectable sum, and take it himself along with representatives of his Churches, he felt confident that there would be a *rapprochement*, and his life's work would be crowned. There can be little doubt that Paul was a martyr to the cause of Christian reunion. How the Gentile Churches as a whole responded to his appeal we have no means of knowing. The Macedonian Churches made a generous contribution (see 2 Cor. viii, 2 ff.), and individuals at Corinth showed much interest (see 1 Cor. xvi, 16) ; Paul's helpers too entered into his plans with zest, but unfortunately Luke is silent about it, and in the interview with James (Acts xxi, 19 ff.), nothing is said on either side about the matter. I am afraid we must conclude that the result was disappointing.

At last Paul is free now to fulfil his ambition, but hindrances strew all his way. Landing at Tyre, he is met by a unanimous appeal from the little group of Christians there not to go on ; apparently Luke joined in the entreaty at Caesarea (Acts xxi, 12), where Agabus prophesies Paul's arrest in words perhaps deliberately reminiscent of similar prophecies about our Lord's journey along the same road (see Mark x, 33 f.). But Paul, like his Master, sets ' his face like a flint,' and they go forward. At an unnamed village between Caesarea and Jerusalem they stop for the night with ' Mnason, an original disciple (of Jesus) ' (Acts xxi, 16 ' Western ' text). It may well be that, as Mnason, who still lived on the road, told the story of the last journey of Jesus, Luke first conceived the idea of using his stay in

Palestine to collect such stories and write a Gospel, bringing out this dramatic parallel between Jesus and Paul.

We need not retell the story of their arrival, and of James's well-meant but unfortunate suggestion that Paul should conciliate Pharisaic opinion in the Church—it is interesting to notice that, according to James, ex-Pharisees constituted an overwhelming majority of the Church in Jerusalem—by undertaking to pay the expenses of four men who had taken a Nazirite vow. It is odd that he refers to the decree of the Council almost as though Paul had never heard of it (Acts xxi, 25). Paul leapt at the chance and, to make his patriotic action as well known as possible, appeared publicly in the Temple on seven successive days. Unhappily one of his companions was a Gentile and they jumped to the conclusion that Paul had taken him into the inner Temple beyond ' the middle wall of partition.' A riot ensued, which ended with his arrest. Two years of im-prisonment follow, only varied by occasional opportunities to preach to Roman governors and a Jewish prince and princess. Throughout it all Paul behaves like the great gentleman he was. At the end of two years he set off at last to Rome, with Luke, carrying his precious manuscript, still in his company. One supreme adventure befell them on the way—we may be glad that the manuscript survived the shipwreck—and the Acts leaves Paul safely ensconced in his lodgings in Rome, still in custody, but able to preach without let or hindrance to all-comers. There can be little doubt that the long-expected trial ended in condemnation and death.

CHAPTER III

THE THINKER

In style, tone, and substance there is a great difference between the Epistles of Paul and his speeches reported in Acts. Except in Romans and Ephesians which are the most formal of his Epistles, Paul seems to be thinking on his feet as he dictates. A good example can be found in his last letter to the Church at Corinth (2 Cor. iii and iv). He is here enjoying the rapture of a great relief ; at last he is free to be himself. He begins chapter iii with a reference to a charge made against him which has now ceased to rankle—the insinuation that he was a self-advertiser. That suggests the testimonial brought by Apollos to Corinth, written by Priscilla and Aquila (Acts xviii, 27), and this in turn the Corinthians themselves as *his* testimonial. From this point his brain leaps to the new covenant, God's testimonial, made with Jeremiah (Jer. xxxi, 33 f.), and its contrast with the tables of stone which Moses brought down from Sinai. Then he remembers that Moses had a veil upon his face, and he suggests that Moses wore it because he did not wish the Israelites to see that the glory was already fading. By contrast the Christian preacher's face is unveiled, for he has caught and been caught by the glory shining down upon him from the 'Master-spirit' of the Crucified Saviour, now risen and glorified. The transfiguring spirit of Almighty God, streaming down upon Him from the Cross has ' lit a flame in his heart, to make him a world-beacon proclaiming the glory of the Creator who first bade light shine out of darkness.' What an extraordinary journey of the mind in a few moments ! At other times, as in Galatians and the heart-broken letter (2 Cor. x, 1—xiii, 12) love, anger, sarcasm come tumbling out at such breathless speed, that (as in 2 Cor. x, 2) we can only pity his amanuensis. In Paul's two speeches, as they are reported in Acts, there are obscurities, but they are not of the same kind ; the argument moves straight on to a goal in view from the beginning.

But these addresses are also strangely un-Pauline in substance. This generalization is least true in the farewell-address to the elders of the Church at Ephesus delivered at Miletus. Here Paul is not so much the missionary as the pastor, talking intimately to his friends, but even here there is no special emphasis upon his favourite themes in the Epistles, the only allusion to the death of Jesus coming in Acts xx, 28. The other full-length speeches attributed to Paul are those delivered at Pisidian Antioch and Athens, one before the Sanhedrin at Jerusalem, one before Felix, and one before Festus and Agrippa. Of the two First Missionary Journey speeches, that delivered at Antioch is reminiscent of part of Peter's address at Pentecost ; only in xiii, 39, is there anything specially ' Pauline.' At Lystra, as at Athens, Paul's address is concerned with what may be called natural religion, but the Lystra speech is only a fragment, like Stephen's, and was interrupted, as was his, by the stoning of the preacher. At Athens ' we also are His offspring ' is not a specifically Christian sentiment ; indeed it is the only place in the New Testament in which all men are called outright children of God. As in Acts ii, 22, Jesus is ' a Man ' (Acts xvii, 31), and there is no reference to the Passion. The speech before the Sanhedrin is autobiographical, that before Felix is a personal apologia, and in Acts xxvi, that part of the speech which is not concerned with

Paul's own history is quite general. Some scholars have inferred that these speeches are Luke's own composition, that, like other ancient historians, he composed addresses which he thought suitable to the occasion, and put them into the mouths of his heroes. But surely they would have been much more fluent in style, if Luke had felt himself free to compose them himself. He can write faultless Hellenistic Greek when he likes (e.g. in Luke i, 1-4). Here he is translating his source, with laborious literalness ; consequently his style is cramped and often obscure. I see no reason for doubting that Luke had notes of Paul's addresses, and, if they are less lively than we should have expected, that is because they are notes. When we read John Wesley's printed sermons, we marvel that such compositions could have set England on fire. Of course, as they have come down to us, they would never have done so. Wesley was a long preacher, and the longest of the sermons as we have them would not have taken more than half an hour to deliver. As they were actually preached, they must have been full of illustration as well as impassioned appeal ; all we have is the skeleton. Paul, too, was a long preacher (Acts xx, 9), but the addresses we have in the Acts are shorter than Wesley's sermons. We cannot believe, however, that in subject-matter Paul's missionary preaching was altogether different from the outlines given in Acts.

When we turn to Paul's own testimony, in his earliest Epistle, our confidence in Luke's trustworthiness is increased. In 1 Thess. i, 9 f., he gives us himself an outline of the content of his first teaching in Macedonia. It runs as follows : ' You know how well our mission in your city began, and how you were converted from idols to worship the living and real God, and to await His Son from Heaven, whom He raised from the dead, Jesus who rescues us from the coming wrath.' His topics, by his own testimony, were monotheism, the Second Advent, the Resurrection of Jesus who is our Saviour from the wrath to come. There is no direct word about the Cross, no reference to faith, or union with Christ; indeed the word 'Christ' does not appear. We infer that there was a common scheme of Christian propaganda to which Paul conformed; the exigencies of his pastoral work in Galatia and his experiences at Athens and Corinth led him to develop his message along the lines we associate with his name. If that is so, we may have to give up the idea that he thought out his doctrines in Arabia or anywhere else; he only became the great thinker he was, because he was compelled to think for his people. All his natural aptitudes were towards energetic action after his conversion as before it. He never dreamed of becoming either theologian or author. If he had been thinking of posterity, Paul would no doubt have been able to make it plain whether Titus was circumcised or not, or— to mention a much more important matter—to what extent he was familiar with the details of our Lord's ministry. But he is writing, not upon Christianity in general, but on particular difficulties which had arisen in his Churches, and we cannot be sure that all his Epistles taken together give us a complete picture of his missionary preaching. In the Epistles written from prison, he has more leisure for reflexion, and his style is noticeably different. Perhaps he wrote them with his own hand; in any case, his pace is slower and he is far less apt to digress. In other letters Paul often seems to have forgotten how he had begun the sentence, and, as he is dictating, does not look back. Sometimes, as in 1 Cor. xiii, and Rom. viii, his familiar prose falls into rhythm, and at the same time finds wings; under the stimulus of a lofty theme, he proves himself a grea

Christian poet. He became an inspired artist, as he became a consummate theologian, but he was neither consciously or deliberately.

In the last chapter I hope to go down to the roots that lay beneath all Paul's thinking as well as all his heroic service, his passionate adoration for his crucified and risen Lord; here I shall take it for granted, but must ask my readers to bear in mind the fact that Paul was never indulging in theological or ethical speculation for its own sake, that he was always trying to discover for himself and his people the application of the fact of Christ to problems of thought and conduct *as they arose*. He began with the crucified and risen Jesus of Nazareth, not with the world or the Church. From that fact he went on to life as he saw it in himself and the world about him, but all his conclusions were based on the one controlling fact, God's action upon his own soul and the souls of his people, in the crucified, risen, and ascended Lord.

First, then, there was the *fact*; he had ' seen Jesus our Lord,' and the Lord who had laid hold of him was the crucified Nazarene. Since he was a Jew of the dispersion, the first word which would come to his lips to describe what Jesus had become was ' Christ.' All the hopes which home and synagogue had made part of his being were centred henceforth in Him. Luke is right when, in Acts ix, 22, he tells us that immediately after his vision on the Damascus road, Saul began to argue with the Jews in the synagogues of Damascus that Jesus was ' the Christ.' When, three years later, he went up to Jerusalem to interview Peter (Gal. i, 18), Peter would tell him of his life with Jesus, and specially of the last night on which Jesus had broken the bread which, He had seemed to say (see p. 83), was 'His body,' and passed round the cup which was ' His blood.' He had told

E

them then that He would come back to them, and eat and drink with them in the Kingdom of God. In Gal. ii, 6 Paul says that the original apostles ' added nothing to him ' ; by this he meant that all that they told him was in line with his own ' revelation ' of the Lord.

In his early ministry, then, Paul was sufficiently occupied in the business of preaching Jesus as Christ. The main burden of his message to Jews is contained in his address in the synagogue at Pisidian Antioch ; Jesus is proved to be the Messiah, God's messenger, Saviour and Judge by His resurrection from the dead ; all the prophecies of Old Testament revelation have been fulfilled in Him. To Gentiles he began, not with the Old Testament, but with the revelation of God in nature and in the longings of the human mind after the divine. Now a Man has appeared, in whom God has once and for all confirmed what His revelation in nature and in the mind and conscience of man foreshadow. This Man has been raised from the dead, and is the appointed Saviour and Judge of all men.

It will be seen that Paul is applying the fact of the risen Christ, who had been Jesus of Nazareth, and is Lord supreme, first of all to his own experience as a law-abiding Jew, with certain ethical ideals and national hopes, quickened and kept alive, but not satisfied, by the Old Testament, then to the moral and religious condition of his fellow-countrymen, and to the lost and hopeless pagan world about him. His diagnosis (Rom. vii, 9 ff.) of his own condition without Christ is as relentless as is his verdict upon the state of the Jewish and Gentile world in which he had been brought up. He is aware of redeeming features in Jewish and Gentile life (Rom. ii, 14 f.), but is sure that, over Jew and Gentile alike, there hangs ' the wrath to come.' But if he insists upon the corruption of the heart of man,

his pessimism is the result of inward and outward experience; it is not the dogma of a theologian, but the conclusion
to which his sensitive spirit had long before been driven.

Dr. C. H. Dodd (in his *Commentary on Romans*), points
out that, when Paul speaks of ' the wrath ' or ' a wrath
of God,' he does not mean that God is angry in the same
sense as, when he speaks of the love of God, he means that
God loves. The ' wrath ' (as in 1 Thess. i, 10, Rom. i,
18) is equivalent to what we should call the moral law of the
universe ; ' things are what they are, and their consequences
will be what they will be ; why should we deceive ourselves ? ' The Jews, because of their furious hatred of and
contempt for foreigners, and the contrast between their pre-
tentions and their conduct (1 Thess. ii, 15 f. ; Rom. ii, 21 f.)
are already involved ; the nation is going down the steep
place to the catastrophe of A.D. 70. But the doom of Gentile
society is also inevitable.

But this is only the dark background to the equally
certain fact that Saul himself and his converts, Jews and
Gentiles alike, had been delivered from the present world of
conscious guilt and impending doom by the shining of the
light which came from the face of the risen and exalted
Christ upon and into their souls, so that they could say
Christ was living in them. They lived the same lives,
walked the same streets, met the same people as before,
but there was Someone within them who looked out
through their eyes, so that everything and every one seemed
different. His power showed itself in varied ways, but they
were conscious that they were not their own men any
longer ; they were possessed. This inner light made them
all the more conscious of darkness without, but two things
were true at least ; they could preach Christ because, when
they opened their mouths to speak, He spoke for them, and

they were no longer alone. The contrast between light within and darkness without might make life a strange riddle ; they might not even fully understand themselves, but at any rate they had the clue which would lead them through the labyrinth ; they would understand when they saw Him face to face who was already the hidden life of their hearts.

I have put all this in the plural, as Paul generally does ; it is characteristic of him that when he is talking of the futility and frustration of life without Christ he says ' I ' ; generally (though not always) when he is speaking of the certainties of Christian experience he says ' We ' (cf. Rom. vii, 9 ff. with viii, 1 ff.). But we must not assume that all his readers had an experience so clear-cut and confident as his ; in his large-hearted charity he takes that for granted. This inward life, this Person living in believers and speaking through them, he calls ' the Spirit ' ; he does not distinguish between ' the Spirit of God,' ' the Spirit of Christ,' and ' the Holy Spirit.' Again, he is severely practical ; he is dealing with facts. Nor does he discuss what or where Jesus was before His appearance at John's Baptism. What He has become and what He is doing for Paul and his fellow-believers so fills his mind that it does not occur to him yet to ask the question : ' What must He have been to start with ? ' That will come later. For the time being Jesus is preached as ' Son of God ' in the sense that He is ' marked out as Son of God because He was endowed with supernatural power and possessed by the spirit of holiness, as Jesus Christ our Lord because of His Resurrection from the dead ' (Rom. i, 3, 4). I think the punctuation I have followed, against most editors, brings out the balance of clauses clearly.

In the Thessalonian Epistles there are only two phrases

which are not covered by the outline of Paul's early preaching given above. One is ' those who were put to sleep by (or ' through ') Jesus ' (1 Thess. iv, 14). We should have expected ' those who fell asleep in Christ,' i.e. Christians who have passed away, after they have experienced the new Christ-controlled life. The phrase reminds us of a saying of Jesus in the Fourth Gospel ' If I go and prepare a place for you, I will come again, and take you to Myself, that where I am, there you may be also ' (John xiv, 3). Perhaps its best explanation can be found if we unite it with the other phrase, ' who died for us ' (1 Thess. v, 10). Paul tells us (1 Cor. xv, 3) that he had ' received ' (from the Church which he joined after his conversion) the doctrine that ' Christ died for our sins according to the Scriptures,' ' the Scriptures ' being, of course, the Old Testament, and the passage in question Isa. liii, 8 f. Perhaps Paul would have put it like this : Christ died, and so opened a way of salvation to us and to the world from the ' coming wrath,' that is, the otherwise inevitable nemesis to which our sin was leading us.

As always, Paul is arguing from a *fact*, the fact that he himself had been delivered from the prison-house of self-despair, ' the body of this death,' by the crucified and risen Jesus. With this deliverance the Passion and the Resurrection were bound up. The next Epistle (Gal. iii, 13 f.) gives us one of Paul's many attempts to explain how this came about, but now we are concerned with the *fact* which had to be explained. Isa. liii, 8, confirmed it, as did also what Peter had told him about the Last Supper, when Jesus had said ' This is My body for you.' (See p. 83.) It is clear that Paul began with the Resurrection, for it was the risen Jesus who had appeared to him, and made his new life of freedom possible. But the Cross which had been his stumbling-block (1 Cor. i, 18), is now seen to contain the clue to the whole mystery of redemption. The full understanding of that mystery would come later, but the fact was certain; Christ died for us, and He died as Son of God; this was proved not only by His life of sinless obedience, but by the fact that God had raised Him from the dead. Moreover, He died a death of extreme humiliation, and He must have gone to death of His own choice. Why? Surely that He might rob death of its sting for those who believe in Him, and, possessed by His Spirit, follow His obedience. For them, since Jesus died, death had become a sleep, and that had been made possible by Jesus. As Saul of Tarsus, Paul had watched Stephen die, and had wondered at his serenity; now he understood. Stephen had seen Jesus standing (Acts vii, 56) and a few minutes later 'had fallen asleep' (vii, 60); Saul had been near enough to see the expression on his face, and had been moved in spite of himself.

In the next Epistle (Galatians) Paul is still thinking out the explanation of the deliverance from hopeless frustration which had come to him, and was coming to so many others, through the death and Resurrection of Jesus, in connexion with an urgent practical problem. He had alarming news from Galatia—the question as to who the 'Galatians' were will be dealt with in a later chapter— Jews masquerading as Christians had persuaded some of his converts that Paul, who was not one of the original apostles, had only told them half the truth. There was a higher and more authentic Christianity, to which the original leaders of the Church—Peter and James, the Lord's brother—conformed; this included circumcision and the observance of Sabbaths and Jewish feast-days. This propaganda was the more attractive inasmuch as it was much more like the ceremonial religion to which these Phrygians were accustomed; Paul's gospel had carried them off their feet at first, but now it seemed somewhat unreal and difficult to grasp.

We saw [1] that a bare doctrine of salvation by works was not characteristic of Pharisaism after the fall of Jerusalem ; the Rabbis taught, if we may judge from their literature, salvation by repentance. But we cannot imagine Paul tilting at windmills ; at any rate, the Jewish propaganda in Galatia must have been taken to imply salvation by works. To allow his converts to fall away into this bastard Judaism was to leave them in the very prison from which Paul himself had escaped. The fact was, as he tells us (Gal. iv, 17), that these Jews were trying to swallow his Churches whole, to let him convert Gentiles from heathenism, and then sweep them over into Judaism. I believe Dr. J. H. Ropes [2] was right when he suggested that there were others in the Churches who not only poured scorn on this propaganda, but wished to throw over the Old Testament altogether, and with it all discipline in the Christian life. So Paul was not only faced with backsliding, but with division in his Churches. One party charged him with being a reactionary, and preaching circumcision (Gal. v, 11), the other with preaching a religion of his own invention.

It was necessary to prove that his message had come direct from the Lord, and to make the issue between the doctrine which had brought deliverance and new life to them and this strange amalgam masquerading as full Christianity perfectly plain. But he had to fight on two fronts ; he still believes that the Old Testament is the word of God, and so, as the Old Testament is the chosen battle-ground, he must justify his position from Scripture itself.

[1] See pp. 15 ff.
[2] In *The Singular Problem of the Epistle to the Galatians*,

Again, he starts from the *fact*; the death and Resurrection of Jesus has actually brought deliverance from moral frustration. This freedom had not come through obedience to 'the law,' for that was just the trouble; even those, like himself, who reverenced the law most, found themselves utterly unable to obey it. No; it came, because they had responded to the revelation of the risen Lord; Paul calls this response 'faith.' But the Old Testament speaks of 'faith'; Abraham was the father of the 'faithful,' because he 'believed' God. His position was founded, not on obedience to law, for the law had not been given yet, but on his response to God's initiative. All God's dealings with man had been begun and carried through not by man's achievement, but by God's revelation of Himself, and man's acceptance of that revelation. Why was the law given at all, then? It came in as a kind of afterthought, an interim arrangement for those of Abraham's descendants who refused to respond to God's overtures, its purpose being to lead them to the impasse in which Paul had found himself, thus making them ready to respond to God's next appeal, the sending of His Son. But there were not two dispensations, but one, and that was of grace, in Old and New Testaments alike; the law was meant to educate the conscience, and so make men ready to accept Christ. To go back from Christ to Moses was like going back from adult life to infancy.

Paul illustrates this distinction between covenant and law by the Greek customs regarding probate and inheritance current in South Galatia. Under Roman law, as under ours, the last will invalidates all previous wills, if it is properly attested. In Greek law, no later will can annul the official will, passed through the record-office of the city and laid up there, in which the citizen is bound to name an heir or heirs to his estate. He must appoint some one to carry on the family and no children born afterwards can dispossess the heir named in this will. Paul has here taken advantage of the fact that the authorized Greek translation of the Hebrew ' berith' (covenant) was a Greek word which usually meant ' will.' The terms of God's covenant were settled by God Himself, and it was meant, not only for Abraham, but his posterity. So the covenant becomes, so to speak, God's will, and the law a codicil added afterwards, but not contradicting earlier arrangements. In the official will, the testator appointed stewards and business-managers, until the heir named in the will came of age, and also settled the time when he should do so.

But now we come to the supreme question, ' What was this consummate revelation to which all the history of God's dealings with nations and with men leads up?' It was Christ crucified, and Paul can never forget how rapturously the Galatians had welcomed it, in spite of the fact that the preacher had not been at his best when he first came to them—Paul is thinking of his physical condition after the stoning at Lystra, I think (Gal. iv, 14)—they had welcomed him as if he were the Lord Himself, and the immediate effect of his message had been amazing (iii. 5). ' O you senseless Galatians, what evil eye has bewitched you, before whose eyes Jesus Christ crucified has been placarded on the hoardings,'[1] (iii, 1). Paul says in effect : ' I'm only a bill-poster, and I came and painted your towns red with a picture, and "every picture tells a story." In any case, the sight of the picture seemed to transform you. Then, when my back was turned, somebody came along and scrawled all over my picture "Moses!" What an outrage! What

---

[1] I owe the thought, and much of the language, of these sentences, as I owe so much else, to Dr. Rendel Harris.

must be the state of mind of people who, after seeing one
picture, can have eyes for any other ? '

'But why had this picture so much power over me, and,
through me, over you ? Because it was the picture of the
Son of God "who loved me, and gave Himself up to this!"
for me and for you. His death was one upon which,
according to His own word, God had set His curse. We
were under a curse, too, for there is a curse upon all who
disobey God's law. This is the law by which the universe
is governed, and the consequences of disobedience, in
which we all knew ourselves to be involved, must be that
we are up against the God-appointed facts of life. This
was not true of Jesus, for He was always obedient, so, as
He did not share one " curse " with us, He put Himself
under the other. " He has redeemed us from one curse
by identifying Himself with another " ' (Gal. iii, 14). This
kind of argument is difficult for the modern mind to
follow ; it seems to make too much of the letter of the
Old Testament. We must remember that Paul believes
it necessary at once to refute those who misread the Old
Testament, and those who wished to set it aside altogether.
The argument about Hagar and Sarah is of the same
type, and need not detain us now. It is clear that Paul
is fighting for the very existence of a Christian Church in
Galatia, and snatches at any means of enforcing his plea,
however far-fetched it may seem to us.

With the party who wished to dispense with law altogether Paul is much more curt (Gal. v, 13 ff.) ; in Romans
he deals more fully with this antinomian tendency. Here
he is content with the assertion that there are two kinds of
life ; one he calls living ' after ' (or ' in ') ' the flesh,' the
other living ' after the spirit.' The two were incompatible ;
a man could not be in two worlds at once. It is true that

' the flesh ' by which he means what we call the lower
nature, including sins of temper as well as animal passion,
is still to be reckoned with, but for the believer the motive-
power, controlling his will, is ' the Spirit.' All the energy
of his personality is drawn into other channels ; he has no
taste either for self-indulgence or contentiousness ; his
animal nature is atrophied, and ceases to trouble him
seriously. If members of the Church are still busy discussing the question ' Why cannot I indulge myself in this or
that ? Has Christ not set me free ? ' or snapping and snarl-
ing at one another, that simply means that they are not
Christians yet. It might seem as if Paul uses the word ' flesh '
in two senses in this Epistle, sometimes for the animal
nature, sometimes for the external obedience to rules and
conventions into which more scrupulous members of his
Churches were relapsing, but it is not so. Whether living in
the flesh manifests itself in one extreme or another : whether
in over-scrupulous adherence to law or lawless self-indulgence ; whether the question is ' Ought I to do this ? ' or
' Why should I not do this ? ' those who are occupied with
these matters are slaves to the outward, and have never
known, or have ceased to know, what possession by the
Spirit means. For Paul himself such questions have no
meaning, for nothing else matters any longer but the Cross
of Christ. He has been crucified with Christ (Gal. ii, 19 ;
vi, 14), and that experience has carried him out of the world,
in which such questions can be asked and need be answered.
He bears the marks of the Lord Jesus, and would not let
himself be pestered with such irrelevancies, if the love of his
Lord had not taught him to be gentle with those who are
weak in the faith. They are his children, and he knows
that he must mother them (Gal. iv, 19) until the new life
come to birth.

The Epistle to the Galatians was obviously written under the stress of strong emotion. But the problems raised in these Churches needed more deliberate treatment. Critical questions in connexion with the Epistle to the Romans will be dealt with in a later chapter ; for the moment I shall take it for granted that it was a letter originally meant for the Church at large, sent later, with a covering note, to Rome. We are concerned with it here as revealing the development of Paul's thinking. In the early chapters Paul paints a picture of the condition of the pagan world almost unrelieved in its gloom, but fully justified by contemporary evidence ; his mind is still under the influence of the argument from the natural creation which he had developed at Athens (Rom. i, 20), but the fact that enlightened Gentiles felt its force only made their condition more deplorable. This contrast between philosophical idealism and actual depravity suggests in every line that Paul is writing from Corinth.

In dramatic contrast to this black picture Paul sets, in iii, 21 ff., the salvation which God has made available for Jew and Gentile alike in Christ. I shall paraphrase this classic passage, for it contains the essence of Paul's thinking about the redeeming power of the Cross. ' But as it is, a new opportunity of deliverance, opened by God's action, has been made available, and the Old Testament bears witness to it. It is originated by God Himself, and is open to all men as soon as they respond to Christ. To all, I say, for there is no distinction between Jew and Gentile ; all alike sinned, and come short of God's ideal for them. But they can be delivered by the free gift of God's grace offered in the redemption achieved by Christ Jesus, whom God exposed to the world's gaze as One who should reconcile men to Himself and one another by the offering of His

ife blood. Thus He proclaimed the truth about Himself
and His purpose for the world ; it was necessary that He
should do so, because the problem presented by man's sin
had not been adequately dealt with. It had not been
dealt with because of His divine patience ; but in the
present crisis of the world's history it was necessary that
He should show Himself at once inflexibly righteous and
able to open a way of salvation to the believer in Jesus.'

The point which Paul is labouring is this : the problem
set to a righteous God by the sin of man had not so far been
solved. To threaten him, as He had threatened in the
prophets with the inevitable consequences of sin, was merci-
ful ; it would have been cruel to keep him in ignorance.
But threatenings and object lessons had all failed. Only
two alternatives were left, so desperate was the condition
of the world. One was to destroy mankind altogether ;
that was impossible to a God of love. The other was to
make a new appeal. We are not to think of this new
intervention as a novel idea, for it had been kept in
reserve from the beginning. God first of all sought to
show us what rebellion against His purpose which is the
law of the universe would inevitably mean *to us*, and then
what it means *to Him*. ' Justification ' is not a pretence,
an amiable fiction by which a righteousness to which we
have no claim is ascribed to us. It is an acquittal on the ground
of one compensating fact, the fact that the sinner, bad as he is,
can still respond to the appeal of dying love. In God's
scheme of values that atones for everything else. The
Cross, then, is God's acid test. If that does not, nothing
else can move men ; soon or late, in this life or another,
every man and every nation is judged by the Cross.

It might be argued that this exposition makes nonsense
of the argument which follows in Chapter iv. Here

Paul seeks to show from the Old Testament that this deliverance is not achieved by any merit on man's part, but is a sheer gift of grace. There might be some substance in the criticism, if the exposition did not make it clear that *the initiative comes from God.* The only thing man has to do is to respond, but that response is an act of the will, and must rise from something already within him. We shall never understand the mind of Paul unless we realize that for him God initiates everything in the spiritual history of man. The Rabbis said, ' Do as much as you can, and God will come the rest of the way.' Paul insisted that God came *all* the way. This is why he never speaks about knowing God, without correcting the phrase to ' is known by God ' (Gal. iv, 9 ; 1 Cor. viii, 2 f.) ; only once or twice of loving Christ, nearly always of Christ's love for us. At every point he insists that we had nothing to do with it in the first instance. If our salvation depended on our own efforts, it would be a hopeless business ; since it is God's business, we can be certain that the fight will end in victory, for God's resources are inexhaustible. That is Paul's gospel, and there is no other.

Another point which Paul seems to labour almost to weariness is that Jew and Gentile stand on an equal footing before God. This seems a truism ; Paul emphasized it because it had come to him as a revelation. Brought up in a pious Jewish home amid pagan surroundings, he had been, as we have seen, from his earliest years impressed by the contrast between home and synagogue on the one hand and the world outside on the other. That his people were God's people had become an axiom ; only long and painful experience could shake his conviction that they were the ' saints ' and that the Gentiles whom he met in the university and the streets were sinners. Occasionally he drops into the old language, as in his heated argument with Peter : ' we being by birth Jews and not Gentile sinners ' (Gal. ii, 15). The belief that the barrier (Eph. ii, 14) was broken down, and that, saved or unsaved, Jews and Gentiles were in the same case, grew upon Paul, until it became almost an obsession.

In Rom. iv, 25, the argument takes a decisive step forward ; this verse should be read in close conjunction with Chapter v. It is usually translated (as by Moffatt) ' who was delivered up to death for our sins, and raised with a view to our justification.' But it is unnatural to take the same preposition (dia) with the same case in two entirely different senses in one sentence. Why not render ' Who was delivered up to death in consequence of our sins, and raised from the dead because we were saved ' God cannot be defeated in the long run, the world *is* redeemed by the death of Jesus ? Humanity will respond to the appeal of the Cross ; God would not have made that appeal if He had not known that it would not fail of its effect. Christ died to redeem us from our sins and the Resurrection is the proof that He has done so. He is the first fruits of redeemed humanity, triumphant over death, with which sin is, to Paul's mind, bound up. All we have to do is to avail ourselves of the fellowship with God opened to us by the Cross ; then we can rejoice even in our troubles because ' the troubles that come shall come to our rescue and hurry us home '—to Him. We have always something still to hope for. Then Paul dwells for a while longer on the love of Christ for sinful men, making a distinction between a ' just ' and a ' good ' man which we can all appreciate, and upon the glorious fact that He is alive for evermore, alive within us and waiting for us at the end of our journey.

There follows a paragraph which shows that the thoughts

of Paul are looking backward as well as forward; here (and again in 1 Cor. xv, 45 ff.) they turn to Adam as the representative man. Adam's fall is a universal fall, because his disobedience passed on to us by heredity a spoiled human nature. The Augustinian doctrine of 'original guilt' is, of course, due to the fact that Latin is a less plastic language than Greek. The Greek words which should be rendered 'inasmuch as all sinned' can only be rendered in Latin by 'in quo,' a phrase which generally means 'in whom.' We did not all sin in Adam, but we are all more liable to sin, because we are descended from Adam, and, as a matter of fact, we have all succumbed; Paul is still dealing with facts. One Jewish writer of Paul's time cries, 'O Adam, what hast thou done?' another 'Every man is the Adam of his own soul' (4 Esdr. vii, 118 ; 2 Bar. liv, 19). Paul agrees with both, though he is nearer to Esdras than Baruch. But he is concerned chiefly with Adam as a foil to Christ; evidently his thought is marching on to the doctrine of Christ's pre-existence and Incarnation. How did Jesus come to be the representative Man, if He was not so to start with? But not until his missionary career is for a while suspended did Paul's thought about the pre-existence of Christ come to flower; there are hints of it in Galatians, Romans, and 1 Corinthians, each more definite than the last, but for the moment he is concerned with the work of Christ. At this point he makes a fine contrast between the two representative men. In the one case we start with an act of disobedience mechanically working out in a lost and doomed race; in the other, with a multitude of transgressions through the perfect obedience of the Second Adam miraculously working out in a redeemed humanity. Here is no theorizing about the origin of evil, but a paean of praise to the Saviour.

In Chapter vi Paul turns to our side of the case, for he has still to deal with people who were taking advantage of the doctrine of free grace to justify their own licence. If God is able, they say, to make even the sin of man redound to His glory, He can neither take our sins very seriously, nor blame us if we go on sinning ; that gives Him all the more opportunity to exercise His miracle of redemption. It is difficult to believe that this objection can have been seriously meant, but Paul takes it seriously. Such men fail altogether to understand the nature of faith. Faith is far from being a mere assent or an emotional surrender ; it involves a change in the directing centre of personality, a revolution as catastrophic as death and resurrection. Paul is, of course, writing to people familiar with sacramental ideas, as most modern Protestants are not. He does not mean merely that the believer ' sometimes thinks about the Cross, and shuts his eyes, and tries to see the cruel nails and crown of thorns, and Jesus crucified for me.' By his response to the Cross the believer's spirit lies open to the power of that ' Master-spirit ' (2 Cor. iii, 17, 18) and God acts upon him in such a way that he is actually crucified, buried, and rises again to a new life in a new world. This really happens because God does it. His baptism, his going down into the water a pagan, and rising out of it a Christian, is all that men's eyes see ; really the old human nature dies and is buried, and a new human nature is born. If that is true, talk about continuing in sin betrays the fact that the men who indulge in it have never had this experience at all.

Then Paul sets out in dramatic contrast his own two lives. The fact that his unregenerate life was one of slavery must not be taken to mean that the law was not divine. As God's law, it was altogether good. But, just because it consisted in a series of rules imposed from outside, it came

F

into collision with the natural rebel lurking in every son of Adam ; the very existence of rules stimulated this rebel within him to break them and his conscience to resent their breaking. Every time the issue of the battle was certain before it had begun, and the worst of it was that his conscience, trained by the law, would not let him sin without remorse ; he was like a living man watching himself die by inches without a drug ; he loathed his disease, but could not be rid of it, because it was himself.

But Jesus lived a life like ours and so redeemed our bodily life ; His sinlessness showed that such slavery was not man's inevitable lot. By His death He had done more than that ; He had made it possible to lose the frustrated selves, of which we are so sick, in Him. When we surrender to Him, He—for He carries the Spirit of God with Him— takes the place of the old rebel in the soul, and leads us on to a resurrection of our mortal bodies. So we are transformed *from inside* ; we become sons of God, led by the Spirit, who is released by the death of Jesus. We are conscious of the change in ourselves, and our certainty of the reality of that change is reinforced by the transformation which we see taking place in the lives of other believers— that is what, it seems to me, ' the Spirit (in the Church) bears witness along with our own spirit ' (Rom. viii, 16) means. So we realize that there is a new family of God on earth, heirs of a new world. The conviction grows upon us that it is all God's doing, that He set His heart upon reinstating us from all eternity, that the whole process of our salvation has been initiated and carried through in all its successive stages by Him,[1] and He will see it through to the end.

It is true that the world in which we live has not changed

---

[1] It should be observed that Paul has nothing to say about predestination to anything but salvation in Rom. viii, 30 f.

with us ; nature is waiting, for the universe is like a gorgeous house all in disorder because the heir to the estate has not come to his senses. The universe is one, and man's sin has affected every part of its life ; when man realizes God's plan for him, nature will share his transfiguration as it has shared his humiliation. This is what we have to hope for, a new race of men in a new world. For the moment, it is true, we cannot escape from contact with a world which does not yet share our inward life ; indeed, we carry the evidence that we must still play our part in its redemption in our imprisoning flesh and bewildered minds, but the Spirit which lies deeper within us expresses for us the longings we cannot put into words, and our very weakness is proof of our union with Christ, for we share His incarnation, and nothing can ever separate us from Him either in our present struggle or our coming satisfaction. As Paul says in another place, we ' bear about in our bodies the dying body of Jesus ; that proves that the risen life of Jesus too shall by and by shine forth in our bodies ' (2 Cor. iv, 10).

To Paul the most tragic fact of the present order was the unbelief of his own fellow-countrymen ; for their salvation he would willingly forfeit his own. Their privileges made the tragedy all the more poignant.[1] I have only space here for an outline of his explanation of this fact, but we must remember that each step of the argument ought to be considered in the light of those which follow. The argument of ix, 22 ff., for instance, is not ' God has made some of His human vessels for destruction,' but ' If He did so, He had a perfect right to do so, and we have no cause for complaint ; but, as a matter of fact, He has not done so.' Paul is anxious to assert two things at the same time, the

---

[1] I am sure that we should read in Rom. ix, 5, ' *whose* is God over all, blessed for evermore.'

unqualified sovereignty of Almighty God, and the fact that, though He might, He has not exercised this sovereignty in an arbitrary way. We proceed, then, to our summary :

(1) God has, from the beginning, as Scripture shows, exercised His unquestionable right of selection.

(2) But it has not been an arbitrary process, for the deciding factor in its application has always been the presence or absence of ' faith,' the acceptance or refusal of His overtures.

(3) It is not true to say that God dealt unfairly with Israel ; they had their chance, and the first chance.

(4) Nor is it true that Israel as a whole has been rejected ; there has always been a righteous remnant, and there is one still.

(5) But it is true that the Gentiles would never have come in large numbers into a Church in which Jews were in an overwhelming majority.

(6) But if most of the Jews have been allowed to remain outside, in order that the Gentiles might come in, that cannot be the end of the story ; God's ultimate purpose must be to bring the Jews, who still are God's people—for He cannot change His mind, though His *methods* may be affected by man's freewill—to realize that they are outside, and so induce them to come in. The Gentiles knew they were lost, and so were willing to be found ; the Jews too must realize that they are lost, and therefore will be left out just long enough to let them realize their condition. *In theory*, then, we must allow that God might admit some and exclude others by His own choice, not because of moral qualities possessed or lacking in His creatures ; *in practice* He has chosen all, and only exercised His right of selection in the choice of the means used to procure their salvation.

The rest of the Epistle is concerned with practical rather than speculative issues, and these are to be dealt with under another heading. This is also true of the greater part of the (four) Epistles to the Corinthians. We shall attempt in this chapter merely to trace the development of Paul's thought on the great themes which we associate with his name, as it reveals itself in the course of these letters.

We have already noticed that it was at Corinth that the subject-matter of Paul's preaching changed ; there he forsook natural for revealed religion in his preaching to Gentiles, and concentrated once and for all upon the Cross and Resurrection of Jesus Christ. In the Epistle in which he makes this statement, he hints that he is now at work upon a philosophy of Redemption ; by that he meant that he is learning to explain everything in God, man, and the universe by the fact of the Cross. That philosophy appears full-orbed in Ephesians and Colossians, also written during Paul's three years at Ephesus. All we need observe here is the fact that in 1 Cor. ii, 6 f. he tells his readers that, if he has not produced his full statement to them, it is not because he has not got it ready, but because they are not ready to receive it.

But, of course, if such forward and backward looking thoughts are moving in Paul's mind, they are bound to break through here and there, however rigidly he refuses to let himself go. In 1 Cor. i, 30 f. ' Christ Jesus ' is said to have become ' wisdom for us from God,' this ' wisdom ' including ' salvation, consecration and redemption.' This is the first clear hint that Paul's mind is turning to the question : ' How is it that God's plan of salvation has come to be identified with the life, death, and Resurrection of the Man Christ Jesus ? ' In the ' Wisdom-literature ' of the Old Testament and Apocrypha ' Wisdom ' is described as having been present with God before creation (see especially

Prov. viii, 22 ff.).   In the document known to scholars as
' M ' (consisting of passages found in the First Gospel
alone) Jesus is represented as identifying His own invitation
to the heavy-laden sons of men with the call of the heavenly
Wisdom (Matt. xi, 28 ff.—cf. also Matt. xxii, 3 ff. with Prov.
ix, 2 ff.), but this tradition grew up in a section of the Jewish-
Christian Church with which Paul had no intimacy.   Its
occurrence here is a sign of the direction in which his mind
is moving ; it is not part of the Christological tradition which
he had received.

In 1 Cor. x, 4, we have a more explicit reference to the
pre-existence of Christ, all the more impressive, inasmuch as it is incidental. ' Now this rock ' (the rock which,
according to Rabbinic tradition, followed the Israelites in
their desert-wanderings), he writes, ' was Christ.'   Moses
obtained water from the rock on two occasions ; it was
inferred that it was from the same rock ; consequently the
rock must have accompanied the people from one place to
the other.   It will be noticed that the Old Testament, not
the desire to produce a complete Christology, set Paul's
mind working on these themes ; the pre-existence of
Christ was an inference from the doctrine, taken for granted
by all Christian teachers, that the Church was the ' Israel of
God ' (Gal. vi, 16), the heir of the first Israel.   There was a
Church before the Incarnation ; it followed that there must
have been a Christ before the birth of Jesus, for there can
be no Church without Christ.   If it seems surprising that
Paul was so slow in making this deduction, it can only
have been because he was too busy with evangelization and
Church-management to work it out.

In 1 Cor. xii, 4 ff. we have the first foreshadowings of the
doctrine of the Trinity in the sequence ' Spirit, Lord, God ' ;
again it is unpremeditated.   In this connexion we ought to

consider the benediction which (in 2 Cor. xiii, 13) closes the whole series of letters to Corinth. I am convinced that this formula (' the grace of our Lord Jesus Christ ') was not invented by Paul, but was already the possession of the Church at large, being used in its liturgies, like 'Maran Atha' (1 Cor. xvi, 22) and the Matthean version of the Lord's prayer. The origins of the doctrine of the Trinity should not indeed be looked for in Paul, but in the memories and hopes of the little group of disciples who had lived with Jesus, who would naturally think of the Spirit bestowed at Pentecost as something (or should we say ' Some one ' ?) different from ' Maran ' (our Lord), whose face and voice and bodily presence were an ineffaceable memory. They had ' another ' Representative of His (I think that is the best rendering of the Greek word ' Paraclete ' in John xiv, 16, because it also fits the same word in 1 John ii, 1) to take His place till He came back, but it was no use pretending that He was not ' Another.' Paul, never having lived with Jesus as they had, would not have been so conscious of the difference between those days and these.

In 1 Cor. xv, 47, ' the Second Man is from Heaven,' the clear statement we have been looking for is forthcoming. How fruitful for the development of Paul's thought was the comparison between the First and Second Adam we have already seen in our study of Rom. v, 12 ff. In that passage Paul was concerned with the work of Christ ; here He is concerned with the nature of His person, and the words ' from Heaven ' introduce a sequence of ideas which lead directly to the doctrine of the Incarnation. In his illuminating book on the Fourth Gospel Odeberg tells us that ' the idea of a high celestial spirit descending into an earthly being was not unknown to Jewish thought. In the second century, A.D. Jewish mystics held that the divine seed of the

First Adam (the "spirit man") forfeited by Adam's fall (when he became "earthy") joined itself with Enoch, Abraham, &c.; this idea was also known by Rabbinic Judaism in the latter part of the first century.' What Jewish thought would not admit was that a man born of earthly parents could himself be of celestial origin; he might become the temporary home of the Spirit, but could not himself be the Spirit (cf. John vi, 41 f.). Christian thought had already learned to think of Jesus as, from His Baptism onward, uniquely endowed with the Spirit; the new idea here suggested and afterwards worked out by Paul is that the pre-existent Christ, the heavenly Man, who had been God's agent in the creation of the world, had supported God's chosen people in the desert with heavenly food and drink, and had inspired the prophets to foretell His own coming in flesh and blood, had actually become incarnate in Jesus. This is perhaps the reason why 'Christ Jesus,' rather than 'Jesus Christ,' Paul's usual formula up to this point, is found more frequently in Paul's later Epistles.

The other subject on which his mind is working is that of the nature of human personality. The 'spirit, soul, and body' of 1 Thess. v, 23, is conventional, and in Romans the terms 'flesh' and 'body' are used interchangeably, as opposed to 'spirit' (cf. vii, 24 with viii, 8). But in the Corinthian letters a new conception of the 'body' as distinct from the 'flesh' appears; it is, as we should have expected, closely connected with the thought of 'the Second Man from Heaven.' Before we make the connexion plain, it will be well to define the meaning of the words 'flesh and blood,' 'body,' 'soul' and 'Spirit' in the later Epistles. By our flesh we are animals, by our bodies we are members of the human race, by our souls we are individual

personalities, and by our Spirits we are related to the divine
Spirit. We have flesh and blood, and so are animals, we
have bodies and so are men, we *have* spirits, and so can
hold communion with God who is Spirit, but we *are* in this
life souls. The distinction between flesh and body is not
easy to grasp, until it is realized that for Paul, who was
more Jew than Greek on this as of most other subjects,
the body included every means by which we communicate
with one another—gestures, handwriting, facial expression,
a light in the eye, as well as speech. This body was composed of flesh and blood, but all bodies need not be ; ' there
are earthly bodies and heavenly bodies.' ' Flesh and blood
cannot inherit the Kingdom of God ' ; they have to do with
this life and this life only. But in that other life we shall
still be members of the human race, so we shall still have
bodies, but they will be ' spiritual bodies,' that is, bodies
communicating our new heavenly life as our bodies of flesh
and blood communicated our old earthly life. Whether the
change from earthly to heavenly takes place gradually in the
sleep which death for the believer has become, or instan-
taneously at the second coming of the Lord (1 Cor. xv, 51 f.),
these spiritual bodies will preserve our identity ; God will
find a way of creating a body which our friends will recognize as ours, more truly our own than our first bodies of
flesh and blood can ever be ; spoiled as they are by the sin
of all those who went before us, and consisting of flesh
doomed to decay, they cannot fully express the Christ-life
within.

What then did Paul mean by ' The body is for the
Lord, and the Lord for the body ' ? (1 Cor. vi, 13.) The
risen body of the Lord, carried our human nature,
body and soul, ' to the clouds at God's right hand ' ;
this glorified body of His is the pledge of the

redemption of our bodies of flesh and blood. The risen body of Jesus was not identified as His by any physical marks except the wounds in hands and side, for two friends of His could walk and talk with Him along a lonely road without recognizing His face or His voice. They recognized Him by characteristic mannerisms, the way in which He broke bread, or folded clothes, or pronounced a woman's name who loved Him. The flesh and blood body, limited by space and time, was gone, but the communicating personality was still there ; He was Jesus of Nazareth still. The wound-prints remained, for they represented what He had made of His body of flesh and blood. We, says Paul, are to ' glorify God in our bodies ' (1 Cor. vi, 20) ; the Spirit possessing us is more and more, as life goes on, to shine through our bodies of flesh and blood, transfiguring the face and harmonizing the voice ; the spiritual body will reproduce in more suitable material what the Spirit has made of our earthly bodies.

' Every sin that a man commits,' says Paul, ' is outside the body, but the fornicator sins against his own body ' (1 Cor. vi, 18). Other sins—Paul is evidently thinking here of such fleshly sins as drunkenness and gluttony—degrade the man himself ; fornication involves another person. The body represents then a complex of social relationships. By sexual intercourse a new ' body '—that is a new social entity—is created ; that is proved by the fact that from such intercourse a child may be born who will belong equally to both parents ; he can never be anything but a child of them *both*. By God's appointment the two who are joined in this way can never be their unrelated selves again in this life, and therefore intercourse with the temple harlot is incompatible with Christ possession. Whether the man who indulges in such intercourse recognizes the fact or not,

enceforward he belongs to the woman whom he uses for
is pleasure, and cannot belong to Christ.

There is another passage in this Epistle in which the word
body ' occurs. Paul tells his readers what he had ' received
rom the Lord ' about ' the night on which He was being
etrayed ' (1 Cor. xi, 23 ff.). The Lord broke the bread and
aid ' Take, eat ; this is My body for you.'[1] This is usually
nterpreted as meaning that the broken bread symbolizes
he body of Jesus broken on the Cross, in spite of the fact
hat the Fourth Gospel insists that the body of the Lord was
ot broken till after death (John xix, 36). If the suggestion
s to the meaning of the word 'Body,' namely, that it means
ot the flesh and blood, but the self-communication of one
oul to another through flesh and blood be accepted, may
ot the body here mean *not* the material flesh of Jesus, but
he act of breaking bread by which His friends at Emmaus
ecognized their risen Lord ? It is as though He said, ' Here
in this familiar gesture) you have My body, all that has
ecome so dear to you because it is inseparably connected
n your minds with Me ; break the bread, because you want
o remind yourselves how I broke the bread.' If that is so,
n the bread we remember the Lord's life, His living presence,
n the cup we remember how that life was laid down. We
hall consider the meaning of the ' blood ' of Jesus in
nother connexion ; for the moment I want to see how far
his interpretation of the word ' body ' will carry us in our
onsideration of the difficult passage which follows. In
Cor. xi, 29, we read, ' He that eateth and drinketh eateth
nd drinketh judgement to Himself, because he does not
stimate the body at its proper value.' If we render 'the
ody ' here as the real presence, we shall not find much
o perplex us. Judas ate and drank with Jesus, but the

[1] This is, I believe, the original reading (without ' broken ').

sacramental bread itself did not save him from judgemen indeed, immediately he received the sop ' Satan enter into him ' (John xiii, 27), because in the Lord's presence could still be thinking of his coming interview with t priests, as if He was not there. Those in the Corinthia Church who treated their fellow-believers with contempt ous discourtesy did not recognize that where bread w broken and the cup passed round, the crucified and ris Lord was present. They were indeed exiling themselv from that presence ; no wonder their very bodies of fles and blood were breaking down, and some of them we dying before their time, when they were guilty of such a outrage upon the Jesus whom they still called Lord ; the were going the way of Judas.

We Christians do not believe merely in the immortali of the soul, but the ' Resurrection of the body.' In th life we are living souls, expressing themselves in bodies flesh and blood ; in that life we shall be not souls, but spirit expressing themselves in bodies *not* of flesh and bloo Paul does not seem to be quite consistent in his use of th word ' soul '; sometimes it stands for the whole ma sometimes for a region between flesh and spirit. Perha this last use of the term ' soul ' (psyche) can be illustrate by a homely figure. It is as though we each lived in a three storeyed house. On the ground floor is the kitchen and th dining-room (the flesh) ; on the first floor the drawing-roor in which we entertain our friends (the social life), a busines office, a picture-gallery (the imagination), a study, and so on this is our psyche. Above that is an upper-room with skylight open to the stars, where, alone or together, we sa our prayers, and hold communion with the Lord. Th man who spends his time on the ground floor is the fleshl man, he who alternates between the two lower levels is th

atural man (literally, the 'psychic,' but not of course in
ae modern sense of the term), the man whose life is
irected from the upper storey is the 'spiritual' man.
He who is joined to the Lord is one spirit' (1 Cor. vi, 17)
aplies that, in Paul's view, the 'Master-spirit' of the
scended Lord (2 Cor. iii, 17 f.) controls the whole of the
eliever's life from the upper chamber, moulding psyche
ad flesh alike to His purpose. At death, according to
ae thought of 1 Cor. xv, 36 ff., psyche and flesh alike
rop away, but the spirit carries on our identity through the
eriod of 'sleep' and is prepared in undistracted com-
aunion with the Lord for its new home, the spiritual body.
hose who are still in this body when the Lord comes again
ill undergo this change in a moment (1 Cor. xv, 51 f.).

In 2 Cor. v, 1 ff. Paul's thoughts on what happens at and
ter death are seen to have changed. He no longer thinks
f a state of 'sleep' intervening between the disappearance
f the old body and the coming to birth of the new. In the
aterval he has been himself very near to death (see 2 Cor.
9), and has come to see that any separation from human
asociations such as this 'sleep' implies is unthinkable. Now
e prefers to think of the *absorption* of the old body in the new.
Ie is conscious that he is living in a slum—we may wonder
ill-health as well as persecution had not something to do
ith this—and, as Dr. Rendel Harris has said,[1] is looking
orward to his removal to better quarters *with immediate
ossession*. Paul's theorizing is always the outcome of
xperience.

But there was probably another reason why he rejects the
lea of a disembodied state intervening between the
eliever's death and the coming of the Lord, and its con-
deration will lead us on to the next landmark in the history

[1] In *As Pants the Hart* (Hodder and Stoughton).

of his thoughts. The idea of the body as a social organism
was growing upon him; 'the bread which we break
does it not represent our common share in the body of
Christ?' he had written (1 Cor. x, 16). Our bodies of
flesh and blood, inadequate as they are, give us the power of
becoming part of the body of Christ, the one 'loaf' of
which we all partake, which is the Church. Even for
period, to be disembodied would mean that we should have
ceased to be members of the Church; we should be separated
from the communion of saints which is 'the blessed company of faithful people' in earth and in heaven. Those
who have already passed away must now possess their
spiritual bodies, and so can communicate with each other
and, in the realm of the spirit, with us.

In the Epistle to the Ephesians lines of thought about
the Cross worked out in Romans and about the relations
between body and spirit worked out in the letters to
Corinth, meet. The Church is the *body* of Christ; the body
of the risen Lord is in Heaven and is the living centre round
which departed saints in their risen bodies gather to worship
and pray for saints on earth. But if His glorified body is in
Heaven, His Spirit is on earth, and has fashioned for itself
an earthly body which is the Church. By this body He
expresses Himself; it is to Him as the organ to the musician
the organ may not be perfect, but the musician is divine
and can mould to His purpose the most refractory materials
In 1 Cor. iii, 9, Paul had said, 'You are God's building,
and in iii, 17 'you are the temple of the Holy Spirit.' But
there he is thinking of many buildings on one foundation
now (Eph. ii, 20) of one building with 'Jesus Christ' as
'the chief corner-stone.' The individual believer's body
is the Temple of the Holy Spirit in 1 Corinthians; now the
Church as a whole is the Temple.

But how are believers drawn out of the world into this body ? The answer is ' by the blood of Christ ' (Eph. ii, 13). I have gone through all the references to the ' blood ' of Christ in the New Testament, and have come to the conclusion that wherever it is spoken of, it has to do with the bond that binds us to one another as well as to Him. The clearest case of all is 1 John i, 7 : ' we have fellowship with one another, and the blood of Jesus Christ His Son cleanses us from all sin' : but the words of Jesus Himself, reported in 1 Cor. xi, 25, are almost equally explicit ; there He speaks of ' the new covenant sealed by My blood ' (or perhaps, ' brought into being by My blood '). Moses made the twelve tribes of Israel into one people by sprinkling them, all alike with ' the blood of the covenant.' Now they were not merely henceforth a people, but a covenant-people (we should say a 'Church'), because that which brought them and kept them together was not their common tastes or antagonisms, or even their common blood, but God. Jesus, by shedding His blood, has made a new Israel, a second covenant-people ; the marvel of it is that in this new Church Jew and Gentile meet, the tie between them overriding their age-long antipathy. This is Paul's supreme mystery ; we shall see how the attempt to realize it in practice filled his mind more and more. We are brought into the body of Christ, then, by His blood, and deeper than all our antagonisms and divisions is the call of the blood. We may lash out at one another as we like, but we shall be brought together ; we did not forge the bonds that bind us, and cannot break them. We may not care about Christian Reunion—it is, with the rank and file of our Churches the least popular of all good causes—but all the things we do care about—world evangelization, social redemption, world peace—depend upon the accomplishment of this.   What really matters to us is what matters to God, and revelation is unmistakable on this point ; He died that ' all God's children who are scattered abroad may be brought into one ' (John xi, 52) ; in this matter the whole New Testament speaks with one voice, and we do well to listen.

' Till we grow to *one* perfect Man, to the measure of the full growth of the Christ ' (Eph. iv, 13) ; there we have the consummation of Paul's long experience.   Is the world ever to be won ? Yes, but only when there is a new in-carnation.   That new incarnation is impossible in our divided Church ; how can we imagine a divided Jesus ? We may, if we like, think of the consummation of unity in Heaven, since it seems unattainable on earth ; but that is to give up this world in despair.   Individuals are being won by the testimony of individual Christian experience, but it is not enough to save individuals, for an unsaved world is ruining men faster than we can save them.   Society as a whole can only be saved by the Spirit of Christ working through the one body which shares His sufferings and carries to its goal His redemptive work.

In the Epistle to the Colossians Paul takes up a suggestion thrown out, but not developed, in Rom. viii, 19 ff.   We are not concerned here with the exact nature of the heresy which was troubling the Church at Colossae ; it is enough to say that it had to do with an idea which haunted the ancient world, an idea which Paul could understand because he had shared it, and only conquered it by the love which had cast out his fear.   He was a child of his age ; if he had not been so, he could not have appealed to it so power-fully.   He had brooded long over the moral condition of the world, which had been an obsession with him before his conversion.   Was it true that it was cut off from God by malignant powers dwelling in some intermediate sphere between earth and heaven ? Was there a ' prince of the power of the air ' (Eph. ii, 2) exercising his tyranny over the minds of men ? If there was not, how account for the fact that, with all men's longings for purity, in spite of all the human decency which he found on every hand, civilization was sinking ever deeper into corruption ? Jesus had explained the presence of the tares among the wheat by the intervention of an ' enemy ' who had come into the field of human life from outside, and though He was not afraid as Paul had been, had warned us to ' fear him who, after he hath killed, can destroy soul and body in hell ' (Matt. x, 28) —surely He meant the devil, not God !

We have the same misgiving as we watch the nations, all longing for security and peace, yet lurching heavily down the steep place to another catastrophe, which no one wants, a nd no one knows how to prevent. Are we under a spell ? This idea haunted Paul's imagination, but he believed that these hostile forces had been conquered first by the Cross, in which God had come down to men, identifying Himself so closely with their strange destiny that no hostile power could ever come between, and then by the Ascension. They had not been able to prevent Him coming down or going back again (Col. ii, 15) ; obviously they were helpless now. Helpless to injure believers, yes ; but still they held sway over the great world outside the Church ; the universe was still rent by rebellious powers, groaning in pain ; natural convulsions were only the outward signs of deep disturbance. It was waiting for ' the revelation of the sons of God,' waiting for the Church to finish the redeeming work begun by the Saviour. We have been lifted above the swaying battle and seated ' in the heavenlies ' with Christ, but only in order that, like Him, we may descend and ' fill

G

up what is lacking in the sufferings of Christ' (Col. i, 24), first on behalf of His Church, that she may be one and complete, then for the world, that the Church, having come at last to her own, may by suffering redeem it. Then nature will be herself again, 'very good,' as God made her. The universe came into being by the obedience of the word, God's agent in creation ; then the word became flesh, and lived and died out His obedience ; so men are drawn in their turn by the appeal of the dying love of Jesus, to obey Him as He obeyed the Father. Last of all in their obedience, the obedience of individuals and the obedience of one world-wide society, all men and the universe itself shall be delivered from division and decay. Only obedience which is faith working by love, can redeem, as only obedi-ence can create. So as the universe found its origin, and finds its explanation, it is to find its consummation, in Christ, and His Church.

In the Epistle to the Philippians 'the wheel has come full circle.' In Col. iii, 3, Paul had said, ' your life is hid with Christ in God ' ; now the centre of his interest has passed from earth to heaven. He might have said with Bernard of Clairvaux ' My heart also hath passed from me, that where He is there it may be.' Solitary confinement has left its mark upon him, and he has been dwelling in the heavenlies too long to have any fear left for the Church or the world ; ' He must reign.' For the first time quite explicitly he describes the descent of the Saviour from His ' equality with God ' into time and space, and uses the example of His surrender as the ground of an appeal to imitate His divine humility. A note struck once or twice before (as in 2 Cor. v, 7 f.) rings out clearly now. His task of thinking for his people is finished ; now he can talk to this dearest of all his Churches of his private hopes : ' If I had the choice of life or death I know which I should choose,'[1] other things being equal, he says ; death would be best for me. All his hopes are concentrated on the longing, growing upon him through the years, to see the face of Jesus. Perhaps after all it was best that he should wait a little longer, to stay with them, and he is content either way, and has no fears left either for himself or for them, if they will only love one another, as the Lord had loved them.

I go on to paraphrase the passage in which Paul makes his last appeal for Christian unity, which had become, along with love for the Saviour, the master-passion of his life (Phil. ii, 1 ff.) : ' If there is anything to spur you on in Christ, if loving and being loved by Him has any power to console you, if fellowship in His Spirit means anything at all, if you know what His tender compassion means, make my joy complete by cultivating His point of view, having love like His ; that means keeping the one goal in view, doing nothing in a spirit of petty rivalry or with a view to keeping up appearances, but in real humility thinking the others more important than yourselves. Let each group among you concern itself not merely with its own interests, but with those of all the other groups. Your rule of life should be to follow the example of Christ Jesus, who, though He was divine, did not exploit His equality with God, but surrendered it, and was content with the life of a slave. He was born as others are, and men came to know Him because He was so human ; indeed He followed the path of obedience all the way to death, yes, death upon a Cross. That is why God highly exalted Him, and bestowed upon Him the Name that is above every name, that, when the Name of Jesus is uttered every knee in Heaven, on

[1] Translating ' I do not know which I shall choose,' as ' Which I shall choose, I do not tell you.' (Phil. i, 22.)

earth, beneath the earth, should bow, and every tongue confess that Jesus Christ is Lord supreme, to the glory of God the Father.'

To summarize : Paul began with the *fact* which had changed his own life—that the crucified Jesus of Nazareth had been raised to God's right hand. He had, by His death and resurrection, become Paul's saviour. In the early years of his ministry Paul was so much absorbed in preaching his gospel of salvation that he had little time, and perhaps little disposition, to do anything but testify to his own experience. The exigencies of pastoral work compelled him to systematize his message. For some time he concentrated, as was natural, on the work of Christ, and so was led to consider His person. When that stage was reached, the momentum of his thinking, swayed by adoring love for his Lord, carried him on to the doctrine expounded in the passage I have just paraphrased, and at the same time, and by the same process, to his doctrine of the Church. It was providential that, in the later years of his ministry, his long imprisonments gave him much time for thought. But we shall misunderstand him completely, if we think of him as either theologian or mystic by temperament ; his findings were the inevitable results of his own experience interpreted by an ever-deepening love for his Lord.

CHAPTER IV

THE PASTOR AND LETTER-WRITER

In each of his Epistles Paul is concerned, not merely or even chiefly with doctrine, but also with Christian conduct. This is less true of Romans and Ephesians than of the others, but what we should call the ' application ' has a large place assigned to it even there.

Ephesians might conceivably have been written by some one else ; Galatians and the Corinthian Epistles could not ; they have Paul's personality written all over them. Our best method of procedure will be to take the Epistles *seriatim*, bring out the chief features of each, in so far as they have not been discussed in the last chapter, and use the materials we have collected to build up a portrait of Paul as the pastor of his Churches.

It is clear that Paul recognized two authorities ; they were ' the Scripture ' (by which he means our Old Testament) and ' the Lord.' By ' the Lord ' he probably meant some collection of the sayings of Jesus of the same general type, though not perhaps so extensive in range, as was the document which seems to underlie the non-Marcan sayings of Jesus common to the First and Third Gospels (called by scholars ' *Q* '). Perhaps it would be well to pick out sayings definitely ascribed to ' the Lord ' in the Epistles. They are :

1 Thess, iv, 15, ' This we say—it is a word of the Lord—that we who live on to the Second Coming shall not rise before those who are asleep ; for the Lord Himself shall come down from Heaven with a bugle-call, with an archangel's voice and God's trumpet-blast and the dead in Christ shall

rise first.' It is difficult to say where this question of priority is even alluded to in the Gospels; the nearest parallel is Matt. xxiv, 30, 31, but this is not very close, and the question ' Who shall rise first?' is not dealt with. Rom. xiv, 14, ' I know, and am persuaded in the Lord Jesus,' is another case, referring, I think, to the teaching underlying Mark vii.

1 Cor. vii, 10, ' To the already married I command— not I, but the Lord—that a wife should not be divorced from her husband, and, if she is already divorced, let her remain unmarried or be reconciled to her husband, and a man is not to divorce his wife.' This instance is all the more striking, because in the next verse Paul says, ' I, not the Lord.' Paul is a strong witness in favour of the version of this saying found in Mark x, 11 f.; Luke xvi, 18.

1 Cor. ix, 14, ' So also the Lord commanded that they who preach the gospel should live of the gospel ' (Matt. x, 10; Luke x, 7).

To these instances should perhaps be added 1 Cor. xi, 23; ' I received from the Lord what also I handed on to you,' that the Lord Jesus, ' on the night on which He was being betrayed,' &c. This should probably be rendered ' as coming from the Lord.' It has been suggested in the last chapter that the information came from Peter. If we extend our survey to the speeches of Paul in Acts, we must also include ' Remember the words of the Lord Jesus, how He Himself said "It is more blessed to give than to receive," ' (Acts xx, 35). This is nowhere to be found in the Synoptic Gospels.

When we consider how highly Paul valued a ' word of the Lord '—he quite clearly regards a saying of Jesus as the last word on any question, leaving nothing more to be said —it is disappointing that the formula ' the Lord said ' occurs so seldom, and it has been argued that Paul cannot have known much about the days of the Lord's flesh ; if he had, he would surely have quoted Him oftener. But there are many more coincidences between sayings of Paul and sayings of Jesus, and they can scarcely be fortuitous.

Our inference should be that there are few direct quotations, not because Paul was not familiar with the sayings and doings of Jesus, but because there did not often happen to be a text which could be applied directly to a particular difficulty.

First Thessalonians.

Paul and Silas (see above p. 40) had seemed to run away from Thessalonica, and the chief purpose of the First Epistle, sent from Corinth, was to defend the character of the missionaries. Many of their converts (Acts xvii, 4) were married women, whose husbands were still heathen. Capital had been made of the fact that the preachers had twice over (Phil. iv, 16) received a present of money from Philippi, their last preaching-place before they came to Thessalonica, and it would be suggested that these Jewish charlatans made a habit of coming to a place, getting round women who had more money than sense, and then, when it became too hot to hold them, running away and leaving their dupes to face the music. What they really wanted was a contribution to be sent after them to the next town ! It might be thought by people unacquainted with the facts that Paul and Silas' behaviour had lent some colour to these insinuations, and Paul sends this message by Timothy, at once to vindicate his character and encourage the flock who felt themselves deserted by their shepherd, and were altogether having a bad time. The difficulty was that Paul could not tell the whole story without inculpating

Jason, his host, and he is too chivalrous to do that; he is content to say that 'Satan' prevented him coming to Thessalonica (1 Thess. ii, 18) and trust them to understand.

But there was another reason for writing. The Thessalonians had been greatly excited by his preaching of the Second Coming (1 Thess. i, 10), and some of them had actually given up their occupations, and were spending their time in discussing when He would arrive. Paul bids them ' make a point of avoiding religious hysteria, and going on quietly with their business ' (1 Thess. iv, 11). The fact that some members of the Church had already passed away caused depression; their relatives were tempted to think that, if they had been real Christians, they would have been kept alive till He came. There is a good deal of local colour in this affectionate and lively letter. We have a picture of the night-life of a Greek city in 1 Thess. v, 7, affected no doubt by Paul's observations at Corinth, and stern warnings against dishonesty and unchastity, the two characteristic vices of the cities of Greece.

Second Thessalonians.

The authenticity of this letter has been widely doubted; its tone is more formal, less cordial. But there seems no valid reason for suspicion. In *The Earlier Epistles of Paul* (Kirsopp Lake) the suggestion was made that Paul had reason to fear that the First Epistle might not be read by the whole Church (1 Thess. v, 27). Evidently Jewish and Gentile Church members were not habitually meeting together, and there was at least one question which concerned the Jews only which called for immediate treatment. The Jewish world was then in a great state of excitement. Some years before this the mad emperor Caligula had conceived the idea of setting up his statue in the Temple.

The statue was actually made, and was conveyed to Ptolemais, the chief port for Palestine. On various pretexts the governor of the province kept it there for nearly two years. At last Caligula insisted on its being moved on, and while it was on its way, to everyone's relief, Caligula was murdered. The Jews all over the world took this as a sign that the Anti-Christ was dead, that the end of the world had come. Apparently, Timothy reported on his return to Paul that Jewish members of the Thessalonian Church were infected by the mood of the moment. On this theory 'the man of lawlessness' still to come is Nero, who, of course, had not yet come to the throne, and 'the restrainer' Claudius, who called the whole business of the statue off.

But Paul is not likely to have spoken of an emperor still to come as the 'man of lawlessness'; his attitude to the Roman government is defined by Rom. xiii, 1 ff., and by his later appeal to Caesar, who was to be Nero himself. While the Caligula story indicates the mood of the time, it seems to be much more probable that by 'the man of lawlessness' is meant extreme Jewish nationalism, the enemy which Jesus fought literally to the death; it was, throughout the whole of this period, obviously driving the nation to ruin. 1 Thess. ii, 15 f., shows us how much this was on Paul's mind at this time. The 'restrainer' was the moderate party among the Pharisees, but that was being 'removed,' for the Rabbis were during this period going over one by one to the popular side. A collision with Rome was certain, and could have only one result. As a matter of fact, the zealots did take refuge in the Holy Place during the last weeks before the city finally fell and perished in the flames which reduced the Temple to ashes. So Paul's prophecy was literally fulfilled.

It is interesting to notice that messages and even letters

purporting to come from Paul were already in circulation
(2 Thess. ii, 2), and that he is anxious that the Church should
be familiar with his signature (2 Thess. iii, 17).　I think we
may accept the letter as genuine on the basis of this argument
first put forward by Harnack.　Timothy brought back news
that Jewish and Gentile Christians were meeting separately
at Thessalonica, and that unhealthy excitement was specially
rife in the Jewish meeting.　It is worth while mentioning
that the much-quoted text ' If any man will not work,
neither let him eat ' (2 Thess. iii, 10) does *not* mean that idle
people must be allowed to starve to death, but that they
must not be kept *at the expense of the Church*.　There is a
characteristic Pauline epigram in 2 Thess. iii, 11, ' not
working, but working round,' or, as Moffatt translates ' not
busy men, but busybodies.'

Galatians.

Something has been said in the last chapter about the
reasons which prompted Paul to write this Epistle.　Here
we must ask the question: ' Who were the Galatians ? '
For centuries the belief was universal that they were the
inhabitants of the country which, ever since the invasion
of Greece and the northern half of Asia Minor by the Gauls
in the third century B.C. had been called ' Galatia.'　It was
supposed that when Paul said (Gal. iv, 13) ' You know that
because of ill-health I preached to you at first,' he meant that
his course had been deflected from Asia into this district,
and that he took the opportunity to found Churches in its
cities (Ancyra, Pessinus and Tavium).　As a matter of
fact, we hear nothing of the existence of Churches in this
district till much later, though it may be argued on the
basis of 1 Peter i, 1, that there were Christians in North
Galatia in the first century, for in that passage ' Galatia '

comes between Pontus and Cappadocia, and North Galatia in fact did so.

Sir William Ramsay put an entirely different construction upon the whole problem when he published his *Historical Commentary on the Galatians*. He argued: (1) The name Galatia was applied to a much larger area in Paul's time, when the kingdom of Antiochus of Commagene and part of Phrygia (including Lycaonia) was included in the province of Galatia. It seems much more likely that Paul wrote the Epistle to the Churches in the southern part of the province. That he established Churches in Ancyra, &c., is a pure hypothesis prompted by the misinterpretation of the name ' Galatians '; but we know from the Acts that he evangelized Pisidian Antioch, Iconium, Lystra, and Derbe, all of which belonged to Southern Galatia.

(2) If Paul was ill, the very worst thing he could have done was to turn north-east into North Galatia; the country was thinly populated, roads were bad, and journeys between the great cities almost impossible for an invalid. The central plateau on the slopes of which these cities lay was comparatively healthy and civilized.

(3) Certain illustrations mentioned in the last chapter would be meaningless in North Galatia, where, so far as laws of probate were concerned, Roman legal customs were observed. In South Galatia, on the other hand, the Romans had not disturbed the old Greek-Syrian usage, according to which the official will—passed through the record-office of the city (Gal. iii, 17)—could not be altered by a subsequent arrangement.

Many other arguments might be adduced in support of this view, but it is enough to say that all travellers intimately acquainted with the geography of Asia Minor at first hand hold the ' South Galatian ' theory. It will be obvious how much point is given to ' ye received me as an angel ' (Gal. iv, 14), if Lystra was one of the towns to which the letter was addressed, for we remember how he was called at Lystra 'Hermes,' the messenger ('angel') of the gods.

We infer, then, that the Epistle was written to the Churches evangelized on the First, and revisited on the Second Missionary Journey. A good deal has been said about the question which was agitating Paul's mind when he wrot the letter as well as about the argument of the Epistle in two previous chapters (pp. 27 ff., 62 ff.).

Paul's argument in the account of his attack upon Peter (Gal. ii, 11 ff.) is not very clear. It would seem to run as follows : ' If you, being a Jew, live like a Gentile and not like a Jew, why are you bringing pressure upon the Gentiles to become Jews ? Both of us are by birth Jews, and not " sinners " like these Gentiles, but we know that a man, Jew or Gentile, is saved from his sins, not by obedience to torah, but by faith in Christ Jesus ; and we believed in Christ Jesus . . . But if, because we sought salvation in Christ, even we ourselves came to be regarded as " sinners," has Christ involved us in sin ? The idea is preposterous.' Evidently the argument turns upon the meaning of the word ' sinner.' Paul takes it for granted that Peter agrees with him, and suggests that by withdrawing themselves, Barnabas and he were undoing the effect of their previous action. Peter was such an important person that easily-impressed Gentile converts would be led by his example to imagine that after all the old distinction between Jew and Gentile had a meaning ; if there was to be a high table, and Peter preferred to sit at it, the distinction which his previous action had seemed to deny would be made permanent, and Gentiles would aspire to become Jews in order to qualify to sit with Peter.

There are other obscurities in this chapter. As we have seen (p. 33), we cannot be sure whether or no Titus was circumcised. The question is complicated by a various reading in ii, 5, where the Western authorities read, ' to whom we yielded for an hour, in a spirit of respectful submission,' leaving out the words, 'no, not.' If they are right, the whole section (beginning at ii, 3) might be read : ' But, if Titus, my companion, who was a Greek, was circumcised, no pressure was brought upon him by me to submit to it ; but I allowed it in deference to brethren who had no real standing in the Church—I did not find this out till afterwards —who had wormed their way into the meeting to take advantage of the frankness which we have a right to use in Christ Jesus (that is, "as Christian men "), their object being to bring us into their power. We gave way to them for a moment in a spirit of courteous deference, because we were anxious that no one should be able to cast aspersions in your hearing on our behaviour as ministers of the gospel.' If this interpretation is allowable, it would mean that Paul feels he has been let down by his desire to show proper respect to the Church at Jerusalem, and that these interlopers have got under his guard, so to speak. He has been deceived, not by the real leaders of the Church—their behaviour on that occasion was irreproachable—but by people who got his confidence on false pretences, masquerading as leaders. The difficulty I have with this interpretation is the fact that it would be in the interest of so many Church officials in the next generation to leave out the vital words ' no, not,' in order to avoid any suggestion that Paul did not defer to the authority of the older apostles. With the same intention, Romanist scholars still try to prove that Peter and ' Cephas ' were two different people. We must remember that Paul was not writing for our benefit, but to readers who would already be aware of the facts ; what he is anxious about is not to tell the Galatians what happened, but explain how it happened.

The Epistle as a whole gives us the impression of having been written very hurriedly ; it is somewhat jerky and disconnected.   In both the passages we have been considering sentences are begun, but are never properly finished ; but it is this very incoherence that gives it unique value in our eyes. In one place Paul allows himself a savage joke : ' I wish,' he says, ' these people who upset you would cut themselves off altogether, while they are so busy with their cutting ' (Gal. v, 12).   But there are many revelations of Paul's tenderness, and we prefer to dwell on them.   All disputes are forgotten when Paul says, ' I have been crucified with Christ ' ; ' I carry branded in my body the wound-prints of the Lord Jesus,' when he speaks of ' faith set in motion by love,' and bids his people ' Bear one another's burdens, and so you shall fulfill the law of Christ,' when he contradicts his boyhood's prayer clause by clause in the words (Gal. iii, 28)[1] ' in Christ there is neither Jew nor Greek, neither bound nor free, neither male nor female.'   But he is most moving when the passion of his soul breaks out in ' God forbid that I should glory, save in the Cross of our Lord Jesus Christ ' and snatches his pen from the amanuensis to write his postscript in ' big letters.'   Great allowances must be made for a man who is fighting for his life, and we love Paul the more for his passionate outbursts.

Romans.

As was the case with Galatians, most of the subject-matter of this Epistle has been dealt with already.   The

---

[1] ' My God, I thank Thee I was not born a Gentile, but a Jew, not a slave, but a freeman, not a woman, but a man.'

fact that the majority of MSS. have the ' doxology ' (Rom. xvi, 25 ff.) at the end of Chapter xiv, while some few have it in both places, that the Latin version originally lacked xv, xvi, 1–24, and that some texts omit 'in Rome' in Chapters i, 7 and 15, has suggested to many scholars that the Epistle was first written as a statement of Paul's gospel, with special reference to the Jew and Gentile question, for the benefit of the Church at large, and was afterwards sent along with a covering letter (Rom. xv) to the Church at Rome. It is widely held also that Chapter xvi (1-24) contains a testimonial sent with Phoebe the deaconess to *Ephesus* not Rome.

Dr. C. H. Dodd has pointed out with great force that xv, 1–13 is closely connected with xiv, 23, and that xiv, 23 is a most unlikely close for a circular letter, even with the addition of a doxology. Other possibilities are that Marcion, who made a New Testament of his own from a bowdlerized version of Luke's Gospel along with the Epistles of Paul (excluding the Pastoral Epistles), cut out Chapter xv, because of its Old Testament quotations ; he tried, as is well known, to get the Old Testament out of the New. But Chapters x and xi are quite as full of texts from the Old Testament, and there seems to be no special reason why he should have used his blue pencil just here. His anti-semitism might make him object to the statement (xv, 8) that ' Christ was minister of the circumcision,' but he could easily have excised that without cutting away several pages ! Dr. Dodd thinks that the shorter version was an abbreviation made later ; ' if we ask why the cut was made at xiv, 23, there is perhaps no answer but the illimitable stupidity of editors.' I confess I am unconvinced.

As to the destination of Chapter xvi, 1-24, everything seems to me to point to Ephesus. Paul had never visited

Rome, and it seems unlikely that he could have had so many friends there. Priscilla and Aquila are the first on the list, and are mentioned with special warmth as having saved his life. They had been left at Ephesus (Acts xviii, 19), are referred to in 1 Cor. xvi, 19, as sending a message to Corinth, where they had been Church-leaders ; 1 Corinthians was written from Ephesus. They had been originally expelled from Rome (Acts xviii, 2) ; is it at all likely that they would have found their way back ? Moreover, in another charming touch, Paul speaks of the mother of Rufus as having mothered him too (Rom. xvi, 13). She was probably the wife of Simon of Cyrene (Mark xv, 21) ; where had she mothered Paul, if she were living in Rome, and he had never been there ? I agree with Denney that vv. 25-27 cannot have been written by Paul ; it is a very artificial composition, and is probably the work of the editor responsible for the shorter version, if Dr. Dodd is right, or, if he is not right, was tacked on to the original circular letter to give it an ending. If it be asked, ' How did this little testimonial reach Rome ? ' the answer is that all roads led to Rome then, as all roads lead now.

Apart from the doctrinal argument which covers the greater part of the Epistle, and had been discussed in the last chapter, its chief interest is to be found in the scheme of Christian ethics worked out by Paul in Chapters xii and xiii. Here he is free to apply his gospel to practical life without needing to deal with particular local problems. It is interesting to see how closely his code of Christian conduct approximates to that laid down in the Sermon on the Mount, of which there is no reason to suppose he had ever heard. He begins : ' I exhort you then, brethren, by God's infinite compassion for you, to offer your whole lives as a living sacrifice, acceptable to God ; this is true spiritual worship (cf. John iv, 24). And do not let your outward life follow this world's fashions, but let your natures be transformed by the renewal of your inward life, so that you may discover for yourselves what the will of God is, that which means your good, is well-pleasing to Him, and is altogether perfect.'

Perseverance in self-forgetting service is the keynote of the rest of the chapter, with special emphasis upon humility, the ground of all Christian virtue. In xii, 19 ff. he would surely have quoted ' Resist not the evil one ' and ' Love your enemies,' if he had known these injunctions ; we feel that they would have been more suitable than Paul's text from Proverbs. ' Give place unto wrath ' means ' Leave justice to work out its own ends,' and is nearer to the spirit of Luke xviii, 7, than Matt. v, 39 ff. Even more unmistakably than Jesus, Paul counsels submission to the government ; his nearest approach to the actual words of the Lord comes in xiii, 9 (cf. Matt. xxii, 39 f.).

A very interesting question is discussed in Chapter xiv. To us ' The Kingdom of God is not eating and drinking ' is a truism, but all ancient religions, including Judaism, agreed that diet was all-important, because the easiest way for evil spirits to make their abode in men was to get into some animal first, and then induce them to eat the animal. Indigestion was a kind of demon-possession, and vegetarianism a matter of religious, not merely one of hygienic, concern. Many early Christians felt about the eating of meat as Mr. Gandhi feels, or as most modern Christians think of indulgence in alcoholic liquor. Paul is entirely free from scruples on the matter, and regards it, like the allied question of sabbath observance, as a question of conscience. If a man feels that one day is more sacred than another, or that it is sinful to eat meat, he must stand

H

by his conviction; if he has no stop in his mind in either direction, he is no worse a Christian for that, unless he breaks the law of love by trying to prevail upon his more scrupulous fellow-believer to go against his conscience. ' None of us lives to himself ' ; there is no such thing as independence. ' Life is nothing else than the outward-journey of the soul to meet its fellow-souls, death nothing else than the return journey of the soul to meet its God, and *these two are one* ' (Ruysbroeck). ' Whatever is not of faith is sin,' says Paul ; in these matters there is no absolute right or wrong ; anything is wrong for you which you cannot do, without hurting your own or someone else's conscience. Christian liberty must be qualified by Christian love.

The Corinthian Epistles.

The four letters Paul wrote to the Church at Corinth are of enthralling interest. No great soul has ever been revealed as his has been in this correspondence ; in his life and death battle for this Church, Paul has laid bare all his innermost hopes and fears. It was not that he liked talking about himself ; normally he was a reticent man, and the feeling grows upon us as we read that all this self-vindication went sadly against the grain. But, as he says, ' you compelled me ' (2 Cor. xii, 11); we cannot be sorry that they did.

Paul spent eighteen months at Corinth, and afterward went on to Ephesus ; after a short stay there, he sailed to Caesarea, travelling thence to Antioch and back to Ephesus again. During his three years in that city, he found it necessary to write a letter to Corinth about marriages with non-Christians and social intercourse with outsiders generally. In 1 Cor. v, 9, he refers to that letter. It is thought by most scholars that we have part of that letter in 2 Cor. vi, 14—vii, 1. Every one who reads that passage must feel that 2 Cor. vi, 14 has no connexion with vi, 13, and that vii, 2 has still less coherence with vii, 1. If we take vi, 14—vii, 1 away, we read (beginning at vi, 11): 'I am taking you into my confidence' (this is what 'our mouth is open to you' means, cf. Matt. v, 2), 'Corinthians; I am laying bare my inmost feelings. You talk about narrowness of mind; all the lack of confidence is on your side. Now, "fair exchange is no robbery." You see I am using children's talk; open your hearts wide to me. Make room for me; I wronged nobody . . . ' On the other hand, vi, 14 is concerned not with an intimate exchange of confidence, but with heathen marriages, and the question of intercourse with pagans is continued up to vii, 1. The case seems to be clear; how a loose sheet from the first letter got mixed up with the fourth we cannot say; perhaps the Corinthians did not keep the apostle's letters very carefully. An odd sheet might easily have been kept in the Church box by itself, and afterwards included in the last letter by some not very intelligent copyist.

J. Weiss suggested that other parts of this first letter might be found in 1 Corinthians. He pointed out that, whereas in x, 14 ff. Church members are forbidden to accept invitations to meals in idol temples at all, in x, 27 we read 'If any one of the unbelievers invites you, and you care to go, eat all that is set before you, asking no questions on conscientious grounds.' His inference was that x, 1-22, comes from the first letter, and that Paul modified his prohibition in his second letter in view of the fact that it was impracticable in Corinth to avoid intercourse with the heathen altogether; that would mean coming 'out of the world' (1 Cor. v, 10). Perhaps a better explanation of this seeming inconsistency would be to suggest that in x, 14-22, Paul is speaking of invitations to idol temples, in x, 27 of meals in *private houses*.

In reply to this letter Paul received a letter from Corinth, brought probably by Stephanas and his friends (1 Cor. xvi, 17), asking various questions and giving assurances of loyalty (1 Cor. xi, 2). At the same time he heard disquieting news about the state of the Church from members of the ' household of Chloe ' who were visiting Ephesus. There were cliques with rival party cries, there was a very serious case of incest, and the guilty man was still in Church membership. Moreover, Christians had got into the habit of going to law with one another, and there were many disorders in the conduct of worship and at the meals which members of the Church took together. The questions which were asked in the letter from Corinth did not deal with these subjects, but with sex-relations generally and marriage in particular, meat sacrificed to idols, and the relative value of spiritual gifts. All these topics urgently needed treatment (vii, 1, 25 ; viii, 1 ; xii, 1) ; Paul was aware also that strange ideas about the life after death were held by some Church members (xv, 12), he is anxious about his collection (xvi, 1), and wishes to send a message about Apollos (xvi, 12). These topics give us an outline of 1 Corinthians.

As to the exact constitution of the parties at Corinth, we cannot be certain. 1 Cor. i, 12 would naturally be taken to mean that they were associated with the names of Paul, Apollos, Cephas (Peter) and Christ, if it were not that in iv, 6 Paul says : ' I camouflaged the real facts under the names of myself and Apollos for your sakes.' The verb used here everywhere else means ' disguise,' as in 2 Cor. xi, 14, and Chrysostom says that, just as a nurse or mother will taste nasty medicine herself, in order to induce a fretful child to take it, so Paul uses himself and Apollos as stalking-horses for the real party leaders. I am still inclined to think, how-ever, that there were four cliques, the slogans of which are quoted in i, 12, and that iv, 11 has not to do with the general question of the parties at all—for neither Cephas nor Christ is mentioned—but with the secondary question as to whether he and Apollos were, as some had suggested, jealous of each other. He had for the nonce assumed a rivalry, which, as a matter of fact, did not exist, in order by a concrete case to show the stupidity of invidious comparisons between Church leaders.

Some scholars think that there were not four parties, but three, at Corinth. It would be just like Paul to write : ' Individual Church members say " I am Paul's man," " I am for Apollos," " I am for Cephas," but I (Paul) am for Christ ! ' Or, perhaps, the words might have been originally a note pencilled in the margin by a pious reader, and after-wards incorporated into the text. But 2 Cor. x, 7, suggests that there was really a Christ party, and that they gave more trouble than any of the others ! We may reconstruct the situation like this. Apollos had gone to Corinth with a testimonial from Priscilla and Aquila (cf. Acts xviii, 27 (Paul makes a sly reference to this testimonial in 2 Cor. iii, 1 : ' Do I need, *like some people who shall be nameless*, testimonials to you or from you ? ') and his preaching made a sensation. Some members appreciated his addresses so highly that they compared him with Paul to the latter's disadvantage, whereupon others loudly asserted their loyalty to the original founder of the Church. Whether Peter had ever been to Corinth we do not know, but his was a name to conjure with everywhere, and others were inclined to say that neither Paul nor Apollos were real apostles ; Peter (they called him ' Cephas,' his Aramaic name, in order to get the real Jerusalem flavour) was their hero, for he had lived with

Jesus Himself.   Last of all, there were others who ' went one better ' ; nothing less than Christ Himself would do for them.

It is clear from the early chapters of 1 Corinthians that this party business was mixed up with a comparison between Paul's simple gospel preaching and Apollos's philosophical discourses.   He came from Alexandria, and was ' an eloquent Old Testament preacher ' (Acts xviii, 24 f.) of an impassioned type.   Probably he interpreted the Old Testament allegorically in the Philonic manner, and the Corinthians were impressed.   Many of them had been converted from gross paganism (1 Cor. vi, 10 f.), and, since they had amended their lives, had made money and acquired a smattering of culture, of which they were inordinately proud (iv, 8).   Whether they understood Apollos or not, his treatment of these subjects flattered them ; many Church members still do not in their hearts think a minister a good preacher, if they can always understand what he is talking about.

Paul deals ironically with this situation ; his argument is two-fold :

(1) He could have given them a philosophy of revelation ; if he did not do so, it was not because he did not possess one, but that he had more urgent things to do, when he came to Corinth.   They needed saving, and only the preaching of the Cross could save them.   So he preached the Cross, and kept further theological instruction for a future occasion.

(2) It was stupid conceit on their part to think that they could assess the relative merits of preachers and missionaries, as if they were candidates for their approval !   Each had his place, for all built on the same foundation, and the day of judgement, not the ebb and flow of reputation, would test the value of their work.

From this personal matter Paul passes on to a more serious matter—the case of incest. What makes their assumption of the right to put their leaders in their places all the more ridiculous is that it is notorious (v, 1) that a gross case of immorality among their members is disregarded by the Church. Paul proceeds solemnly to excommunicate the man concerned, and clearly believes that exclusion from Church membership will entail the offender's death. Perhaps he was ill already, and cutting him off from the healing ministries carried on by gifted Church members (xii, 28) would mean that his illness would be fatal. It is difficult to believe that ' for the destruction of his flesh ' (v, 5) can mean anything less than death ; if we render ' for the destruction of his sinful passion,' it is not easy to see how turning him out of the Church into the life of Corinth could cure him of that. It would seem that Paul thought that he would stand a better chance in the other world than in Corinth ; ' that his spirit may be saved in the day of the Lord ' can mean nothing less than this. The sentence is not vengeful, but is conceived of as being in the best interests of the man himself. In any case, his presence in Church membership is an intolerable outrage. As it was passover-time, let them purge out the old leaven, and keep the feast of Easter, for ' Christ is our paschal Lamb.'

Turning next to the vicious habit of going to law with one another, Paul ironically suggests that, if they have anybody in the Church upon whom other Church members look down, they should appoint them as arbitrators on finance. By ' the unjust ' (vi, 1) he does not imply that Roman magistrates are corrupt, but that they were out of place as judges in disputes between Christians. Then Paul goes on to make surprising charges against some of his readers ; they were robbing and defrauding their brethren

(vi, 5).   A list of criminal practices follows, with the significant words : ' one or other of these things some of you
were,' but you should have left your old ways behind long
ago ! This passage throws a lurid light on the moral
condition of the Church at Corinth, and suggests that there
was some ground for the fears expressed by leaders at
Jerusalem that the inrush of converts from heathenism
might lower the tone of the Church.

After Paul has spoken his mind on these scandalous
abuses, party strife, toleration of gross immorality, and the
habit of litigation, he goes on in quieter vein to answer their
questions.   He makes no secret of his own preference
for celibacy, but knows he has the best of all authority for
insisting that wives shall not leave husbands, or husbands
wives.   Separation is allowable, so long as it is only for a
time, that the parties concerned may have leisure for prayer.
Here Paul is in strong contrast with Peter, who takes it for
granted that Christian husbands and wives will pray together (1 Peter iii, 7).   I cannot help feeling that Peter
with his ' fellow-partakers in the life of grace ' is a safer
guide in regard to Christian marriage than Paul ; the latter
was not able to hold the balance quite evenly.   We must
respect him, however, for his candour in confessing his
predilections.   But ' It is better to marry than to burn with
desire ' (1 Cor. vii, 9) does not suggest a very lofty view of
married life.   Here again, we may be allowed a comparison,
this time with Jesus.   In Matt. xix, 11 f., Jesus tells us that
there are three good reasons why men and women should
remain unmarried ; they are physical disability, economic
incapacity, and religious vocation.   But the point is that
Jesus regards the married life as the God-appointed norm
for all but exceptional people.   He makes allowances for
those who must remain single ; Paul, on the other hand,

makes allowances for those who must marry. There is a difference in outlook here. ' If you must *marry*, you are none the worse for it,' says Paul. ' If you must *remain unmarried*, you are none the worse for it,' says Jesus. Paul himself seems to be half-conscious of the difference ; there is no mistake about the difference in his tone, when he says ' Not I, but the Lord,' and when he says, ' I, not the Lord ' (vii, 10, 12).

The directions, which follow, however, are so full of common sense that they deserve to be given in detail. Beginning at vii, 12 we render : ' To all the others, I say— not " the Lord " this time—if any Christian man has a heathen wife, and she consents to go on living with him, he must not send her away, and so with the Christian woman who has a heathen husband, willing to live with her ; she is not to send him away. For the heathen husband shares his Christian's wife's consecration, and vice versa ; otherwise, the children would be pagan, but, as it is, they belong to Christ.' I think vii, 16 should follow vii, 14; it certainly seems to do so in sense. So we continue : ' For how do you know whether you will not save your husband, you Christian woman, and, you man, whether you will not save your wife ? But if the heathen partner wishes to go, let him (or her) go ; the Christian man or woman is not bound in that case; God has called you to live a life of peace' (vii, 15, there would be no peace if the heathen partner was *compelled* to stay). The general rule is : ' Let every one continue to live the life God has assigned to Him, remaining where he was at his conversion.'

In vii, 21 we have a famous difficulty ; commentators are about equally divided between ' Were you a slave when you were converted ? Do not worry about that ; but, if you do get a chance of freedom, you will be well advised to avail

yourself of it,' and ' Even if you can become free, rather
remain a slave.' ' Don't become (by your own choice) slaves
of men,' suggests the first rendering, for to refuse enfranchise-
ment would mean *becoming* a slave of men ; the whole
tenor of the passage rather tends to confirm the second.
On the whole, I am inclined to think that the first rendering
is right, and that v. 21, like v. 15, states an exception to the
general rule, that Christians should remain as they are.

In the next paragraph Paul applies this rule to marriage :
the Christian is not to contemplate either marriage or divorce
if he is married already.   The reason is this : ' The present
world is drawing to an end, and the acceptance of new and
distracting responsibilities is therefore undesirable.'   Paul
does not want, he explains, to inveigle his readers into taking
a vow of celibacy, but to help them to sit at the feet of the
Lord without distraction ; the coincidence of language with
the story of Martha and Mary (Luke x, 38 ff.) is remarkable.

A passage follows which has been traditionally expounded
as referring to fathers and guardians who have charge of
marriageable daughters.   This interpretation has to meet
at least two serious objections :

(1) Would Paul have spoken as though a parent or guard-
ian had absolute power to decide whether his daughter or
ward should marry or not ?

(2) If this is what he means, why say, ' But the man of
firm purpose who has made up his mind, who is under no
compulsion, and is master of his own desire ' ?   It cannot be
said to be a very heroic thing to refuse to let a young couple
get married !   The crux is, How are we to translate the word
rendered by the A.V. ' give in marriage ' ?   It has been
shown that it can also mean ' marry,' and this makes sense
of the whole passage.   So we render : ' If any man feels
he is behaving improperly towards ' (or ' is in danger of

misconducting himself with ') ' his girl-friend, if his passions are strong ' (or ' if she is getting past her prime ') ' and it obviously must be so, then let him do what he wants ; let them get married, it is no sin for him. But the man of firm purpose who has made up his mind, and has no pressure put upon him (by the girl), and is determined to keep her as she is, his "spiritual bride"—that man will be doing the ideal thing. Both are right, whether they marry or refrain, but he who does not marry is taking the preferable course.' We may well imagine that the streets of Corinth at night—Christian meetings were held in the evening— would be dangerous for a young woman to pass through on her way to and from Christian meetings. A young man would constitute himself her escort, and the pair would become friendly. Obviously, this would create a delicate situation, and Paul gives the best possible advice, not concealing his own preference for celibacy, but at the same time not pressing it too far.

From this question Paul turns to another difficulty at Corinth : what about meat offered to idols ? A little explanation will help here. It was believed that the air was full of evil spirits ; we should call them germs. The danger of infection from these 'demons' was specially present in the carcasses of animals killed for human consumption. To guard against this danger, it was customary to sacrifice part of the animal in the temple of a deity believed to be good ; the whole carcass then became immune, and could afterwards be consumed on the premises, or exposed for sale in the market, with a guarantee—which would enhance its value—that it was disinfected in this way. A witty Indian missionary told me once that the most noticeable difference between the Englishman and the Hindu was that the Englishman's public house was his temple, and the Hindu's

Temple was his public house.   All cafés in Corinth would
be dedicated to one or other of these gods, and, when you
asked a friend to dinner, you asked him to meet you there
at such and such a time.   The invitation—several examples
of such documents are in existence—would be phrased :
‘ So-and-so invites so-and-so to the table of the lord Serapis
. . . at 3 p.m. next Friday afternoon.’   Trade-guilds held
their meetings at these places under the patronage of their
god.

Two questions were involved. Were Church members to
go to these at all ? Paul says decidedly ‘ No.’   In 1 Cor. viii,
we have a kind of dialogue between Paul and the Corinthians.
It should be explained that there were two opinions on the
question ; one group (? The ‘ Christ party ’) asserted that,
as ‘ spiritual men,’ they were free to go where they liked, and
that this idea that ‘ idols ’ had any real existence was a bogey
with no terrors for the enlightened.   Having been initiated
into the Christian mystery, they were immune.   Probably
the letter from Corinth to Paul stated their point of view,
with which they expected Paul, the champion of Christian
liberty, to agree.   ‘ You ask about things sacrificed to idols,’
Paul says, ‘ I know what you say, we all have knowledge ’
(that is, ‘ we are enlightened people’).   ‘ I say : “ Knowledge
breeds conceit, love makes character.   If any one thinks
he has got to the end of his education, he hasn’t really
begun it ; if a man loves God, that proves that God knows
him.”   About eating this meat, then, I know what you say :
“ An idol has no real existence in God’s universe, and there
is no God but one.   For even though there are many so-
called gods in Heaven and on earth, as there are “ many gods
and many lords,” yet for Christians there is but one God—
the Father—from whom comes the universe, and we are in
Him, and one Lord—Jesus Christ—through whom the

universe came into being, and we owe our life in God to Him ' (the Corinthians were always ready to repeat their creed).

Paul answers, ' All this is true, but you must recognize the fact that not everybody is as enlightened as you are. There are some who cannot get out of their minds the associations with idolatry to which they have been so long accustomed, and their sensitive conscience is hurt. It is perfectly true, as you say, "What we eat will not ensure God's favour; if we abstain we do not feel any loss, and if we indulge, we are none the better for it." But the point is this : Supposing a man sees you, whom he regards as an enlightened person, quite at home in one of these places, will he not be en-couraged—fine edification this !—to ignore the prickings of his conscience, and to join with you in eating, and so your more sensitive fellow-Christian is demoralized by your " knowledge "—your brother for whom Christ died.'

There are many points of interest in this passage. One is that Paul suggests that all real knowledge of God depends upon His first ' knowing ' us, another that, as he has said in Rom. xiv, 23, we are never to override conscience, God's sentinel within, giving us warning that what might be allowable to another man is not right for us. In these matters there is no absolute standard of right and wrong, but, if a stop in the mind makes us hesitate, we must obey it, because it is the voice of God. So Paul sums up the matter, ' If what I eat is going to upset my brother, I will never eat meat again, as long as the world lasts.'

There is a difficulty here, but its consideration is deferred for a moment, while Paul asserts his right to lay down the law in this way. His apostolic status has been questioned because he worked for his living, as Peter and James did not. His definition of an apostle is ' One who has seen the risen

Lord.' If further proof were needed, the existence of a Church at Corinth provided it. Possibly the Peter party—whom Peter would have disowned—were making invidious comparisons.

Peter and James, they would say, are real apostles ; Paul and Barnabas are laymen, and confess their inferiority inasmuch as they do not expect the Church to keep them. That stress was laid upon the fact that Peter and James were married, and took about their wives with them suggests that the critics with whom Paul is concerned here were Jewish Christians who thought of celibacy as a disqualification for ecclesiastical office. In his defence Paul declares first that all the apostles have a right to maintenance by the Churches to which they minister and supports his assertion from the Old Testament, as well as from a saying of ' the Lord.' There were two reasons why he had not availed himself of this unquestionable right at Corinth. One was that he knew his people. His experience at Thessalonica, where capital had been made of the fact that he had received money from Philippi, had taught him that, in the degenerate Greece of that day, it was well to keep as independent as possible. In Palestine a holy man is expected to receive the offerings of the faithful, but Greece was infested by peripatetic lecturers whose fees had brought the profession of religious teacher into contempt. So, following his practice of being ' all things to all men,' Paul refused to take anything at all in Corinth. He would not even act as treasurer of the fund the collection of which he was organizing all through this period ; in 2 Cor. viii, 20, he tells them why. Reflexions were being made upon his integrity ; the only way to be quite sure that people who could not understand why he did not accept money could not hint that he was taking a commission on the collection was to make it unmistakably clear that he had not handled the money himself (cf. also 1 Cor. xvi, 2).

But Paul had another reason; he regarded the almost inhumanly strenuous life he was living as valuable self-discipline. 'I knock myself about and keep my body under,' he says, ' lest after preaching to others, I myself should be disqualified.' In the 10th chapter Paul turns again to the broad-minded party and warns them that they, too, may be disqualified. Participation in the Christian mysteries will not save them, any more than it saved the first Israel who had their sacraments, and yet failed to enter the promised land. The paragraph that follows has been dealt with in another chapter. It ends with the statement that, though idols have no real existence, yet the temples where they were worshipped were haunted by spiritual powers of evil which were very much alive. There were real presences there; communion with Serapis was incompatible with communion with Christ.

All the same there was some ground for the attitude of the latitudinarians. It was not *wrong* in itself to go to these restaurants, but it was certainly inadvisable for more than one reason; even if it were true that an enlightened Christian might take no harm, he must consider the interests of his fellow Church member. On the other hand, Christians would only make their lives in Corinth a misery by morbid scrupulosity; there was no need for the Christian housewife to be afraid of meat sold in the butchers' market. But, if her attention were drawn to the fact that any particular joint had been consecrated in the Temple, she had better not buy it, not for her own sake—it would do her household no harm—but for the sake of the informer, who was watching to see what she would do. In the same way, if a Christian received an invitation to a private house, and wanted to go, he should not ask questions about his food ; but, if his host, knowing he was a Christian, mentioned what had been done with it before it came to table, he should abstain for his sake.   A modern example, which is not as frivolous as it sounds, might be found without much difficulty.   What if a convinced total abstainer is asked out to supper, and suspects there is something in the trifle ? Paul would tell him to ask no questions, and only abstain if his hostess draws attention to it !

To this rule of liberty tempered by respect for the scruples of other people, there is, of course, one serious objection. It is put by Paul himself in the words, ' Why should my liberty be at the mercy of another man's conscience ? ' (1 Cor. x, 29.) Are we, in other words, to abstain from anything that might conceivably offend any one in the Church to which we belong ?   If there is one non-smoker who thinks smoking wrong in a company, are all the others to abstain for the sake of one ?   Of course, we cannot expect Paul to deal with all possible cases.   Perhaps the right answer would be ' No ; but do not smoke in his presence.   If he goes out of his way to find cause of offence, that is his business, but there is no need to flaunt one's own freedom from that particular scruple in his company.'   ' Do all to the glory of God ' (1 Cor. x, 31) means ' In everything remember you are God's people, and that involves avoiding all needless offence to anybody and everybody.'

Among other things, the Corinthians had told Paul that ' they remembered him well, and tried to carry out his instructions exactly.'   But he has some further instructions to give, before he passes on to their next question, ' about spiritual gifts.'   At this point we suddenly lose touch with him, and are reminded sharply that it is impossible completely to modernize him.   In an inspired moment he had old the Galatians (Gal. iii, 28) that ' in Christ ' all social, national, and even sex-differences had been obliterated. He had to pay dearly for his epigrams (as he did, later, for ' all things to all men '), and he heard on good authority that Christian women were causing scandal inside and outside the Church by the freedom of their behaviour. It is, I confess, almost impossible to reconcile the tone of this passage with Gal. iii, 28 ; I think Schweitzer has made the best attempt. We must remember that Paul believed in the Old Testament as the word of God ; he never dreamed of correcting it, as Jesus did. In discussing the sex-question, Jesus pointedly ignored the story of the creation of woman from Adam's side, preferring Gen. i, 27, to Gen. ii, 21 ff. Of course, the two passages contradict one another, and come from different sources. Schweitzer suggests that the Old Testament forced Paul to believe that man in the God-created *order of nature* was nearer to God than woman. In deal *the order of grace* might be said to have superseded the order of nature, but, as long as this world endured, Christians had to live in Corinth as well as in heaven, and must observe what Paul believed were God's appointments for this world. We can easily understand why it was necessary for women to wear a veil of some sort in the Church as well as in the street ; it is only when the apostle, in his usual fashion, seeks to ground a very sensible instruction on the letter of the Old Testament that we get uneasy. To have the hair cut off or even shaved with a razor was the punishment meted out to the adulteress ; on the other hand a man who wore long hair was suspected of unmanly vices.

In xi, 10, we lose Paul altogether, and I am greatly tempted to accept a conjectural emendation of the text. Generally speaking, I am sceptical about such emendations, for it does not seem likely that amid the thousands of MSS. and

I

versions, the true reading could have been missed altogether
But here the mistake may have been made by the amanuensis
in the first instance ; this could easily have happened with
so rapid a speaker as Paul.   A slight change of two words
makes the text read : ' For this reason a woman when she
goes out of the Church (or "to Church") ought to have a
veil on her head, because of the mobs in the street.'

The other instruction Paul has to give his readers concerns
their behaviour at the common meal.   Whether the display
of bad manners which he condemns was due to the parties
referred to in Chapter 1 may be doubted ; the distinction
seems here not to be between the partisans of particular
Church-leaders, but between rich and poor, and was all
the more disgraceful for that reason.   This passage also has
been fully dealt with in the last chapter.   All that need be
observed here is that in xi, 34, we have the first suggestion
of the separation of the common meal and the eucharist in
Church history.

At last Paul is free to turn to the question of ' spiritual
gifts.'   He begins with a reference to the mystery-cults
into which many Christians had been initiated before their
conversion ; each cult had its watchword, by the use of
which initiates could make themselves known to each other
the Christian watchword is ' Jesus is Lord.'   But within
the company of those who make that confession, there are
many diversities of gifts, though the same power lies behind
them all.   He then classifies these gifts, arranging them in
pairs.   We may group them as follows (1) theoretical
understanding of what we should call ' theology '; (2) the
power to apply theological truths to practical life ; (3) faith
(4) the power to effect cures by the application of faith
(5) prophecy, that is, the power to receive special message
from the Spirit, and to pass them on to others ; (6) the power

to test the genuineness of such messages; (7) different kinds of ' tongues '; (8) the ability to interpret their meaning. It will be noticed that in each case the constructive gift comes first, its critical or administrative counterpart second. The parable of the body and its members which follows needs no commentary.

The only ' gift ' about which any elucidation seems to be necessary is that of tongues. There were evidently two forms taken by the gift; in xiii, 1 Paul calls them ' tongues of men and angels.' Sometimes, like Peter at Pentecost, Christians were lifted above their peculiarities of thought, speech and language, and were able to make themselves understood by strangers ; this was rare, and was valued by Paul very highly. In my hearing a Durham miner was able in a prayer-meeting to escape from the dialect—in ordinary speech he was almost unintelligible—and pour forth a flood of perfect English perfectly pronounced ; when he rose from his knees, the dialect came back. The other ' gift ' has also been paralleled in modern times, but Paul is much more dubious about its value. Probably the Corinthians were most impressed by the unusual, and thought this gift the most wonderful of all; they called it the power to speak the language of the angels. Sometimes another Church member was able to make sense of this speech, but that was by no means always the case. This phenomenon would be called in medical language paraphasia, and is due to disturbance in the part of the brain which co-ordinates thought and speech under the stress of strong excitement or exceptional strain.

In xii, 28 ff.—xiii, 13, we have Paul's masterpiece. Before we attempt a paraphrase, we may observe the bent of Paul's mind in the fact that the gift which modern Churches tend to put in the first place—that of organizing ability—

comes with him last but one, ' tongues ' coming last of all. Moreover those who work ' miracles ' are placed after ' teachers ' ; we should put them very high up in the list— if we had any. The casual way in which he includes miracle-workers and healers in the list gives us a glimpse of the difference between the modern and the ancient Church. The passage may be paraphrased thus ' God set individuals in the Church, in the first rank apostles, then prophets, then teachers, then workers of miracles (Bentley emended to " pastors "), then healers, helpers, administrators, various kinds of " tongues " ... You are justifiably keen on the higher gifts, but I will show you the best of all possible ways. Though I can make myself intelligible to everybody and unintelligible to anybody, and have no love in my heart, I am no more use than a noisy gong or clanging cymbal. Though I am a prophetic medium, though I am initiated into all God's secrets, and know how to interpret them, though I have all the faith there is, the faith which moves mountains, and have no love, I am no good at all. Yes, if I give away in charity all I possess, if I devote my whole life in glorious self-sacrifice,[1] and have not love, I am none the better for it. Love is as magnanimous in great things as it is easy to deal with in little things, love is not fanatical, does not gush, is not self-conscious, always acts and speaks in good taste, lavishes itself upon the loveless, yet never gets embittered, can never take evil for granted or be satisfied with any compromise with what is wrong, is only gladdened when the truth comes to light. Love's skin is as thick as its heart is tender, it is all believing, all hoping, all enduring ; that is why love never goes bankrupt. As for prophetic revelations, God will find new ways of revealing His purpose ; as for tongues, they shall

[1] Reading (with the R.V. margin) ' that I may glory.'

cease ; as for theological interpretations, nothing is anti-
quated so quickly, for our knowledge is but partial, and
our inspired utterances serve but a temporary purpose.
When what is perfect comes, what is merely partial soon
fades away.   When I was a baby, I talked baby-language,
my world was a baby's, my logic a baby's ; since I have
become a man, the nursery is left behind.   For now we
see by reflected light, and life is a riddle at best ; then we
shall see *Him* face to face.   Now—What we call " knowledge " is knowledge about things, and so is imperfect ; in
that life I shall know Him, as He in this life knew me.   But
even in this bewildering world we have God's trinity of
angels, faith, hope, love, and of these the greatest is love.'
I have sacrificed the rhythm of this passage, in order to
bring out as much as I can see of its inexhaustible meaning.
There are one or two points which ought not to be passed
over in silence.   We have another unmistakable reference
to a saying of Jesus; its form is nearer Matt. xvii, 21 (the
'*Q*' version) than Mark xi, 23, where it is sadly out of
place.   The clauses beginning with the word ' love ' look
like a character sketch of Jesus, and each might be illustrated from the Gospels.   There is an obvious transition
from the gentler to the more virile qualities of our Lord,
and the climax comes when His biography is summed up in
' all believing ' &c.   Jesus first believed in every one ; why,
if He did not, did He say, ' The Kingdom of God is here ' ?
The time came when He could not believe in the mass of
His fellow-countrymen any longer, but still He hoped.
Why, if He did not, did He make His last appeal to Jerusalem on Palm Sunday ?   Then hope died in His heart, but
still He endured to the uttermost on the Cross.   ' Love
never fails ' brings us to Easter Sunday.   The closing
sentences express Paul's deepest longing, as well as

his philosophy of life, and their consideration must be reserved for the last chapter, when we try to delineate 'the man and the saint.'

In Chapter xiv we have a vivid picture of a fellowship meeting at Corinth. Evidently that Church was not troubled with silent members ; we understand, as we read it, why Paul, in his charitable description of his thankfulness to God for the Church (i, 5) puts 'utterance' first in the list of qualities with which it was endowed. But their sense of relative values seriously needed readjustment. 'Prophecy' was a greater gift than 'tongues,' for they had no value unless an interpreter was present. It is interesting to learn that Paul could beat them all in this 'gift,' if he chose to exercise it! Tongues impress outsiders, not always favourably, but prophecy may convert them ; we are given in vv. 24–25 a glimpse of such a conversion. Paul's advice as to the conduct of these meetings is, as usual, full of good sense. 'When you meet all together, every one has a psalm to improvise '—Corinth was ' a nest of singing birds '—' a revelation to make known, an ecstatic utterance to give, some interpretation of such an utterance.' Only two or three of such utterances are to be allowed at a time, and only one interpretation ; conflicting interpretations might lead to unedifying discussion. If no interpreter is present, let the man who is in ecstasy bring his remarks, so far as the rest of the Church is concerned, to a close, and go on talking to himself and to God. A little lower down (xiv, 32) we come to one of Paul's memorable epigrams : ' the spirits of the prophets are under the control of the prophets ' ; the man who is most completely himself is most truly inspired. Trance revelations were fashionable and sought after ; Paul believes that real inspiration does not paralyse or override human faculties, but quickens them.

The first clause of xiv, 33 should be attached to xiv, 32 : 'God is not a God of confusion, but of peace, and this is true in all Christian Churches '; then we should go on to xiv, 36 : ' Or did the word of God originate with you, or reach you only ? ' In other words, ' Do you think you are the only people in the world ? ' Vv. 34, 35 are sadly below the level of the rest of the chapter, and are certainly an intrusion in the text, for three reasons :

(1) What about women who had no Christian husbands ? How could they ' ask their own husbands at home ' ? (2) In xi, 5 Paul has directed that when she ' prays or prophesies,' a woman should wear a veil; would he have first of all told her how she was to behave herself when she speaks in Church, and then forbade her to speak at all ? (3) Textual evidence proves that these unhappy verses should go; they appear in different places in different groups of MSS. and that is always a sign of a marginal note which has been copied in, wherever there happened to be room. Obviously these verses break the sequence between xiv, 33 and 36, and, as they make nonsense anyhow, we may be glad to be rid of them ; it is a relief to find good reasons, apart from our own likes and dislikes, for the conviction that Paul was not guilty of such bathos.

Chapter xv has been dealt with in some detail already and need not detain us long here. It is not easy to see exactly what the objectors at Corinth asserted. Possibly, with ideas carried over into the Church from other mystery-cults, they believed that those who participated in the Christian sacraments were insured against death, becoming immortal. It followed that those Church members who had died were not genuine Christians. Real Christians would live on till the Lord came. We remember how the very word ' resurrection ' was mocked at or misunderstood at Athens ;

Paul's hearers professed to think that ' Anastasis ' (resurrection) was a female goddess. The Greeks believed in immortality (that is, the survival of individuality) but not resurrection (that is, the rebirth of personality). They said with Aeschylus : ' When once the dust has drunk the blood of a man, once he is dead, there is no resurrection,' as some moderns say ' Miracles do not happen.' Paul answers, ' If dead men cannot rise, then Christ did not rise . . . and, if Christ did not rise, you are where you were before you were converted, and we are impostors.' The line of argument need not be followed any further. In his list of appearances of the risen Lord, Mary Magdalene and the two men at Emmaus are omitted, because they were not to be official witnesses, that is, apostles in the technical sense of the term, and the appearance to Paul is described in exactly the same terms as that to Peter or James. Evidently ' abortion of an apostle ' was one of the abusive epithets flung at Paul by his enemies ; he is a 'misshapen little devil,' they would say.

What does ' baptized for the dead ' (xv, 29) mean ? The most rational explanation would seem to be that heathen sons were received into the Church, because they wished to respect the dying wishes of father or mother, who had said ' Meet me in Heaven.'[1] Paul has kept the question of the Resurrection to the last because of its vital importance ; doubts on that subject cut at the very roots of Christian life. At the beginning of the chapter he labours heavily, but, as so often, under the stress of strong emotion, his sentences take wing, and find a natural rhythm ; their resounding defiance to death, so much in Paul's mind during those dangerous years at Ephesus, when for long periods together,

[1] I owe this to my father (G. G. Findlay). See his commentary on the Epistle in the *Expositor's Greek Testament*.

it might come upon him any day (xv, 31), re-echo down the centuries, always associated as they are to most of us with the greatest solo in Handel's *Messiah*.

After the sermon, the collection. Paul wishes the Corinthians to start a kind of envelope-system, and is anxious that the whole business shall be got out of the way before he comes ; his hopes were not fulfilled. He is unusually cool in his references to ' Aquila and Prisca '— for once the lady is called by her stiff formal name, and put behind her husband. I fancy Paul and Priscilla had had a difference of opinion about the behaviour of women in Church meetings ; probably the obstreperous ladies at Corinth quoted her as their example, for she had been one of the original leaders of the Church there (Acts xviii, 1 ff.). Paul quietly puts her in her place, but we are glad to think that she did not stay there. The fact that in Rom. xvi, 3, Paul himself puts her back in front of her husband, and refers in such glowing terms to them both, confirms me in my belief that Rom. xvi was written to the Church at Ephesus long after the rest of the Epistle was written, and after the three critical years there. So the ' little difference ' ended in this great woman playing a prominent part in saving Paul's life ; to such fine issues may the clash of temperaments lead, when great personalities meet !

This richest of all Paul's letters had a poor reception. It was not taken to Corinth by Timothy (1 Cor. xvi, 10) but Paul despatched him by the longer route via Macedonia, while the letter was sent direct (? with Stephanas). Clearly Paul was a little anxious about Timothy's reception, and was not quite certain that he would reach Corinth at all ; he says, ' If he comes.' Timothy was a rather easily-over-awed young man. He did get there, and apparently had a bad time, and brought back more disquieting news. The news was indeed so bad that Paul decided to pay a flying visit (2 Cor. ii, 1) ; he found the Church in a rebellious humour, and was insulted to his face. He retired in high dudgeon, and sent off a heart-broken letter by Titus, who was older and of tougher fibre than Timothy. Scholars are now almost unanimous that we have the whole or part of this heart-broken letter in 2 Cor. x, 1—xiii, 12, and Kennedy has made the attractive suggestion that Paul's friends Priscilla and Aquila were so much distressed by his condition that they wrote to their friends at Corinth ; their letter was not kept, but Paul's was appended to it, and detached when a collection of his Epistles was made. This would account for the absence of greeting from 2 Cor. x, 1, and the emphatic ' Now I Paul ' by contrast with ' my friends.'

The reasons for regarding 2 Cor. x, 1—xiii, 12 as the heart-broken letter must be obvious to any careful reader. In 2 Cor. vii, 16 Paul writes : ' I am glad to say that I have complete confidence in you,' and his final collection-appeal follows in Chapters viii and ix. Is it conceivable that, *after* making friends, he could have set to work to re-open the old sore ? It is unlike him ; indeed, no sane man would have done such a thing. The benediction (2 Cor. xiii, 13) naturally closes the whole correspondence ; whether its original place was at the end of the third or the fourth letter we cannot tell, but it certainly suits vii, 16 perfectly.

It would be well at this point to collect the insinuations made against Paul at Corinth. Of course we must not saddle the whole Church with these slanders ; the trouble was that its atmosphere was such that things like this could be said. The charges were mutually inconsistent, but there is nothing to be surprised at in that for us. The Church was at odds with Paul ; some said one thing and some another, disregarding the fact that many of the accusations cancel one another out. People said (1) That he was not a genuine apostle ; if he was, he would have expected them to keep him, while he was at Corinth. Paul felt this deeply, defends himself calmly in 1 Cor. ix, and more angrily in 2 Cor. xi, 7 ff. (2) That, anyhow, he had ways and means of making money out of them. Paul answers this with biting sarcasm in 2 Cor. xii, 11 ff.

(3) That he was no preacher ; his appearance was unimpressive, and his ' delivery beneath contempt ' (2 Cor. x, 9 ff.). Paul plays with this charge, and owns up to it in 2 Cor. xi, 6, xii, 5.

(4) That he was unscrupulous, ' all things to all men,' as he had said, that he said one thing and meant another. Paul makes a wry face over this suggestion, but did not take it very seriously. ' Well, let that pass,' he says, ' you see what a clever dog I was ; I caught you by my well-known guile ' (2 Cor. xii, 16). Even in the last letter he returns to the charge. A very significant passage is to be found in 2 Cor. i, 17 ff. ; it may be rendered : ' When I expressed this desire did I practise what some people call my " elusiveness " ? Or, to put it in another way, when I make a plan, do I do so in a worldly-wise way, that " Yes," to-day may be " No " to-morrow, if it happens to suit my convenience ? ' The fact that Paul can moralize a little here, perhaps in reminiscence of a saying of Jesus about ' Yes, yes,' ' No, no ' (Matt. v, 33 ff. ; Jas. v, 12), shows that it had ceased to hurt much. But it is no accident that such words as ' guile,' ' make money,' ' adulterate,' are common in these letters (cf. 2 Cor. iv, 2 ; xii, 16 ff.). Corinth was a great business-centre, and some members of the Church knew all the tricks of the trade.

(5) On the other hand, others said that he was a ' fool,' a little mad.

Paul gallantly owns up to this.   He knows he is a fool ; that ought to gratify them, because, being so clever themselves, they enjoyed seeing others make fools of themselves (2 Cor. xi, 1 ff., 16 f. ; xii, 11).   Scarcely anything so endears us to Paul so much as his handsome acknowledgment that he enjoys playing the fool sometimes.   In the last letter to Corinth he makes a great reply to these two charges : ' If I am mad, as some say, God is responsible for that; if I am only too sane, as others say, it is for your sakes ; for the love of Christ has me in its grip ' . . . (2 Cor. v, 13).

(6) He had had no visions to speak of, like those of which more exciting preachers told.   Paul answers this in 2 Cor. xii, 1 ff.

(7) That he was a self-advertiser, always talking about himself.   Paul tells them that they have forced him to do so (2 Cor. x, 18 ; xi, 16 ff. ; xii, 11 ff. 12, 19), and refers to this charge more obliquely in the last letter (2 Cor. iii, 1 ff. ; iv, 2).

(8) That he was good at writing letters, but feeble in the open.   Paul agrees that this may have been true, but promises them that he will be as drastic as any one can desire when he does come (2 Cor. x, 9 f., xii, 20 ; xiii, 2 ff.). It is quite likely that there was a measure of truth in this charge.   When Paul was deeply moved, he may have become inarticulate.   Some of us can join hands with him across the ages, and say ' We understand.'

(9) That he was a ' higher critic,' and destroyed people's simple faith.   Paul alludes to this charge, painfully familiar to most of us, in 2 Cor. x, 4 ; xiii, 10.

(10) That he was an autocrat, and tried to keep his people to himself.   There is a reference to this insinuation— again, only too sadly familiar to the modern minister— in 2 Cor. i, 24 ; x, 14 ff.

I doubt if the most long-suffering modern pastor ever had quite so much to put up with in his Church, but it is comforting to find that primitive Christians were not so much superior to modern Church members as we have sometimes been given to understand.

Particular references to Paul's self-revelation in the heart-broken letter can best be dealt with in the next chapter: ' the man and the saint.' It did its work, but, before Titus came back to report, Paul went through a time of acutely painful suspense. It is likely that he was dangerously ill; we have his own testimony to the fact that during this period he was nearer death than he had ever been before. At one time, like many other good men, he was sorry he had sent the letter. After the crisis was over, he could not wait for Titus, but went to Troas, where he expected to meet him. Titus did not come, and, though an opportunity of mission-ary work was open to him, he could not take advantage of it, ' there was fighting all about me, and fears in my own mind.' So he crossed the water, and met Titus in Macedonia. He brought good news; the Church had rallied to his support and by a majority-vote censured the man who had insulted him. He hastens back to Ephesus, where he writes his last letter to Corinth a letter of warm affection making friends again.[1] The whole story is told by Paul himself in 2 Cor. ii, 1 ff.; vii, 5 ff. He is anxious that they should forgive the offender; ' I have forgiven him already,' he says.

Little more need be said about this most moving of all Paul's letters (2 Cor. i-ix leaving out vi, 13—vii, 1), a com-mentary, if ever there was one, on 1 Cor. xiii. So far as new lines of thought and speculation are concerned, they have been traced in the last chapter; further reflexions on the insight they give us into the finer shades of Paul's character

[1] Some scholars think that the last letter was written from Macedonia.

can be reserved for the next. But we cannot leave the story without a tribute to this extraordinary man. We close the correspondence feeling that Paul has come down out of his stained-glass window and become a living man, an intensely lovable human being.

Ephesians.

This is not strictly speaking a letter at all, nor was it written to, but from, Ephesus, during an imprisonment which followed Paul's return from Corinth. The fact that the best MSS. omit the words ' in Ephesus ' from i, 1. along with the absence of personal greetings at the end of the Epistle, would be enough to raise doubts as to the accuracy of its title ; that Paul could write ' for surely you have *heard of* the way in which the grace of God . . . has worked ' (iii, 2) and ' since I *heard* of the faith in the Lord Jesus which was typical of you ' (i, 15) should convince us, for how could Paul express himself in so general a fashion to a Church with which he was so intimate (see Acts xx, 25).

To whom then was the Epistle written ? Marcion, whom Dr. C. H. Dodd calls that ' eminent but eccentric Nonconformist divine of the second century,' made a collection of Pauline Epistles, and either he or one of his followers wrote prefaces to them which are still extant. Among them appears an Epistle to the Laodiceans, but not one to the Ephesians. We turn to Col. iv, 16 and read : ' And when this letter has been read aloud in your Church, see that it is also read in the Church of the Laodiceans, and that you read also *the letter from Laodicea.*' We infer that Colossians and Ephesians were written about the same time, and were intended to circulate round the three Churches—Colossae, Hierapolis, Laodicea—but in opposite directions, 'Ephesians' beginning its tour at Laodicea, and Colossians at Colossae.

It is quite likely that both documents ultimately found their way back to Ephesus, the capital of the province ; that is why the Epistle we are discussing got its misleading title. None of these Churches had been founded by Paul himself but probably by Epaphroditus—Epaphras for short. So the sentences in Eph. i, 15, iii, 2 ; find a natural explanation; they had only ' heard ' of him, and he had only ' heard ' of them.

Doubts have been expressed as to whether Ephesians can have been written by Paul ; it reminds us at some points of the Fourth Gospel, at others of First Peter. It is exceedingly rhetorical, and its sentences in the first three chapters are intricate and overloaded ; in i, 3–10, we have seven verses in the original without so much as a semi-colon. The Greek preposition meaning ' according to ' is sadly overworked, and synonyms such as ' power,' ' might,' ' strength ' are piled up on one another, until the task of the translator becomes almost impossible. But the concerns with which the writer is occupied are those for which Paul lived and was ready to die, and in the undoubtedly authentic Epistles we have evidence in plenty of his love of superlatives. There is, it seems to me, nothing in the Epistle which is not a development of ideas suggested in his earlier letters ; the difference in style may be accounted for by the fact that he has now won his last fight, and, for the moment set free from the exigencies of Church administration, can let his mind and his pen run on. Moreover, he has now no amanuensis ; his syntax becomes that of a writer rather than that of a speaker.

We have dealt in the last chapter with the leading idea of the Epistle ; here we are concerned with its pastoral admonitions. As its theme is the unity of the Church—Jew and Gentile alike—in the Church which is the body of Christ, its ethical instructions also are dominated by that idea. A

good example can be found in iv, 25 ff. Here we find
rules concerned with truthful speech, anger, honesty and
thrift, clean speech, and the art of living together. A Greek
or English moralist would say ' Do not tell lies ; they are
unworthy of you ; do not lose your temper, you only lower
yourself if you do ; be honest and thrifty, anything else
is incompatible with proper self-respect ; do not indulge
in unclean talk, you only let yourself down, if you do.'
Paul says, ' You must tell the truth, not for your own but
for the other man's sake ; if you must sometimes be angry—
and you must—do not let personal feeling enter into it, for
the devil will come in between you and your fellow-Chris-
tians, if you do ; be honest and thrifty, that you may have
something to give away ; talk clean, that you may leave a
pleasant impression with those who listen to you[1] ; your
rule should be at all costs of self-restraint not to grieve the
Holy Spirit which has bound you together ; that means
avoiding bitterness and temper, wrath and clamour and
slander, with every kind of bad feeling, being kind with one
another, affectionate, forgiving one another.' Here, as
always with Paul, comes the supreme appeal, ' just as God
in Christ forgave you.'

When the writer comes to relations between husbands
and wives, fathers and children, masters and slaves, we feel
surer than ever that he is Paul, because of his limitations
as well as his excellencies. He is never at his best when he
deals with marriage which he does not understand. At the
end of Chapter v, he keeps dragging himself back to marital
relations ; what he is really interested in is the spiritual
marriage between Christ and His Church, ' this is a great

[1] As 'Chreia' (translated in our versions 'need') means in late Greek a
good story or bon mot, perhaps we should render Eph. iv, 29 'Let no filthy
talk . . . but a witty conversation of an improving kind, such as may leave a
pleasant impression.'

mystery, I mean '—he hastens to say—' that which concerns Christ and His Church.' Marriage between the sexes is not a ' great mystery ' ; it is a regrettable necessity for some unfortunate people, and consequently a self-respecting apostle must say something about it—but how glad he is to turn to something else ! Only the Old Testament and his conviction (v. 31) that marriage was God-appointed, together with the remembrance that Jesus took it seriously, kept Paul from saying what he privately thought about it. V. 33 is peculiar from two points of view ; ' husbands are to *love* their wives as they love themselves, and wives are to *reverence* their husbands,' and husbands are commanded, while wives are *asked* ' Please reverence your husbands '—the difference in sureness of touch is unmistakable. It is easy to say that it was not necessary to tell wives to *love* their husbands, or husbands to *fear* their wives—nine out of ten husbands are more afraid of their wives than of anybody else—but Paul does think that men are superior to women ; I should have thought that his women friends would have taught him better ! On masters and slaves Paul is much more satisfying to a modern reader, and on fathers and children he is altogether admirable.

All the other features of the Epistle, not discussed yet, are thoroughly Pauline—the sense of spiritual evil haunting and dominating this world, the prominence given to the Incarnation and Ascension of the Saviour as a conquest of those unseen forces hostile to man, the conviction that we are living in a spiritual world, and that our warfare is, consequently, not with ' flesh and blood ' ; none of these conceptions are novel. One or two passages need some further explanation, however. One of them is iv, 21 ; here, I think, Dr. Anderson Scott is right in his rendering, 'As is actual fact in the case of Jesus.' As Jesus rid Himself of the

K

imprisoning flesh inherited from Adam by His death on the Cross, and so from the power to trouble Him possessed by evil angels and corrupt men, so we must learn how, by union with His death and Resurrection, to put off ' the old human nature with its desires for sinful self-indulgence, and transformed by the Spirit which controls our moral life, put on the new human nature.'

In iv, 26, we come to a saying which, there is good reason to believe, came originally from the lips of Jesus. In an anti-Marcionite dialogue falsely attributed to Origen the Marcionite speaker quotes this verse as a saying of ' the Lord,' as the orthodox speaker does not correct him, we may take it that it was traditionally ascribed to Jesus. It was probably one of Marcion's famous ' contradictions ' between Old and New Testaments. Joshua bade the sun not go down until his *enemies* had been destroyed ; *Jesus* commands us not to let the sun go down, until your *enmities* have been destroyed. The saying is obviously reminiscent of Ps. iv, 5, ' Stand in awe, and sin not ; commune with your own heart upon your bed, and be still ' ; the Septuagint version has ' Be ye angry ' instead of ' Stand in awe.' The Old Testament suggests that the time when a man goes to bed is the time when he should be aware of God, and get right with Him ; the New that it is the time when we ought to have got right with *man* ; these two, of course, are one, and the two together give us the reason why we were taught as children to say our prayers by the bedside.

Two more passages call for brief notice. One is v, 14, which follows a vivid description of the morning after a drunken party in a Greek city. It is probable that Paul is quoting here from an early Christian (probably baptismal) hymn celebrating our Lord's descent into the underworld (cf.

1 Peter iii, 19 ; iv, 6). There are two readings ' Christ shall shine upon thee,' and ' Thou shalt touch the Christ ' ; both are fine, and it is difficult to choose between them. Very charming is the last sentence of the letter : ' Grace be with all those who love our Lord Jesus Christ with a love that knows no decay.'

Colossians and Philemon.

In Colossians Paul has one special pastoral problem to deal with. We have already, in the last chapter, made some reference to the heresy which threatened the Churches to which these circular letters were sent, and I do not propose to enter into an elaborate discussion of its exact nature ; for this I must refer my readers to Lightfoot's great commentary. ' It was held feasible,' he says, 'to grasp at the lower links of the chain which bound earth to heaven, when heaven itself seemed far beyond the reach of man . . . so men might mount the ladder leading up to the throne of God.' Paul's answer is in parts somewhat obscure to us, because the exact nature of the trouble he is dealing with is lost in the mists of antiquity, but his main contention is this : Christ is the only mediator we need or can use, for, in bringing God down to us, He has raised us to God ; powers which exercise their sway between earth and Heaven may still exist—their dominance over the world outside the Church is evident—but they cannot hurt us, any more than they can help us.[1] Our sin made us once their victims, but Christ has made a public mockery of them, and has removed ' the handwriting that was against us '—the evidence of our guilty bondage which we had written with our own hands—nailing it to His Cross. Not only was the

[1] A modern parallel might be found in the discoveries of Natural Science of the vastness of the universe, so formidable to the sensitive imagination.

writing erased, but the document that had once contained it was torn up and cast aside.   Jesus Himself suffered from contact with these powers, but, by dying, made Himself and those who believe in Him free of them.   ' Our true life is now hid safely with Christ in God.'   The explanation of the universe is now—Christ ; all that opposes or has ever opposed Him must pass ; we need not cringe to unseen powers, but, secure in Him, can hold our heads up in a world that is tottering to its fall.   To alter Calverley's translation of a great ode of Horace :

> The fragments of a shivered world
> Shall fall round us still Christ-possessed.

Only we must enter into His sufferings and share His travail, filling up what is lacking (i, 24) in the sufferings of Christ until this world passes, and the Church takes its place ; so all disharmony shall cease, and the universe return to its true life.

As the ethical teaching of the Epistle to the Ephesians is attuned to its leading idea, so also here.   The note of confidence is dominant in Colossians, as the note of corporate unity is dominant is Ephesians.   Christians should be witty, debonair, unafraid (iv, 6) ; there should be an even-tempered serenity in their demeanour, an unhurried fairness in their dealings.   In Ephesians they are bidden to find ecstasy, an escape from themselves and this iron world, not in spiritous but in spiritual excitement, substituting the Christian psalm for the drunken sing-song (v, 18 f.), here (Col. iii, 15 ff.) emphasis is laid rather on the peace of Christ, and singing ' in your hearts.'

In close connexion with Colossians we should read the letter to Philemon, who belonged to Colossae.   He was evidently a convert of Paul's own ; Paul had not been to

Colossae, but Philemon had been to Ephesus, and there the apostle had been responsible for his conversion. His slave Onesimus had stolen some money and run away. He would scarcely have looked Paul up, for it is almost certain that he would have been in attendance on his master when he visited Paul, and the very last thing a slave could have intended to do would be to meet his master's friends, when he ran away to Ephesus. One of Duncan's strongest arguments for the provenance of the Epistles of the imprisonment from Ephesus rather than Rome is the fact that escape to Rome would have involved a very long and expensive journey, including two sea-voyages with the danger of discovery on departure or arrival each time ; whereas Ephesus, the city of the empire, was a good place to hide in, if he kept out of the way of the police. But he had spent his money, got into trouble, and found himself in gaol, and Paul, whom he would recognize, was there, too ! Paul had not forgotten him, and was able to take advantage of the man's remorse. Now, when Onesimus has served his sentence, though Paul himself is not released he is sending him back to his master, no longer useless, but 'useful' (Paul is, of course, playing on the meaning of the name 'Onesimus'), no longer a thieving runaway slave but a Christian brother. Philemon was generous enough in big things, but inclined to be niggardly in little things. So Paul, well aware of his friend's weakness, and anxious to laugh him out of it, solemnly gives him his I.O.U. for the sum Onesimus has stolen, though he mentions, with disarming casualness, that, when all is said and done, the boot is on the other foot, for Philemon owes his soul to Paul ! He tells him too that he intends to stay at Philemon's house when he gets out of prison, and so make a little more out of him ! Of course, the gracious thing would have been for

Philemon to leave Onesimus to look after Paul in prison, as Paul plainly tells him ; we can only hope he did !

Philippians

Apart from the passages discussed in the last chapter, this delightful letter to his best-loved Church is nearly all personal. There is only one critical difficulty connected with it. Phil. iii, 2, seems to have no connexion with iii, 1, and iv, 4 little with iv, 3. On the other hand, if we read straight on from iii, 1 to iv, 4, the sequence is perfect. 'Finally, my brethren, rejoice in the Lord ; to keep on writing the same word to you is no trouble for me, and it is sound advice to you. Rejoice in the Lord always ; yet once again I *will* say it, Rejoice.' It has been suggested that Paul was interrupted by the coming of bad news ; these mischief-makers, the Jews, had been making trouble even at Philippi, and he continues his letter in a different mood. But this suggestion does not account for the obvious connexion between iii, 1 and iv, 4. Does it not seem likely that the Philippians, like the Corinthians, put Paul's letters into the Church box, that the glue which held the papyrus sheets together cracked, with the consequence that the sheets got muddled, and were copied unintelligently ?

In iii, 2—iv, 3, then, we have the whole or part of an earlier letter dating from Paul's fighting period. There is no suggestion in it that the writer was in prison. The tone of biting contempt which permeates iii, 2, is out of keeping with that of i, 18, in which Paul appears to have reached a tranquillity which the machinations of his enemies cannot disturb ; if ' Christ is preached,' he no longer cares very much who the preachers are or what their motives may be. In this earlier letter such serenity is far away. But there is a beautiful humility about iii, 7 ff. : ' But all the things that

were my assets, I have long written off as dead loss in comparison with the surpassing knowledge of Christ Jesus as
my Lord, for whose sake I suffered the loss of them all, and
still think them mere refuse, so long as I can make Christ my
own, and may find my true self in Him, having no longer
any hope of salvation based upon my own obedience to
law, but one made possible through faith in Christ, made
available to me by God, and depending upon my faith.   My
hope is that I may know Him and the power of His Resurrection, that I may share His sufferings, that my life may
become like His death, and so I too may struggle through to
a resurrection from death like His.   Brethren, I do not
mean that I got there when I was converted, or have even
yet reached my goal, but I press on hoping some day to
make Him my own, even as Christ Jesus made me His own
for ever then.'

Little remains to be said about the last letter to Philippi, as
I have already paraphrased the great Christological passage
in ii, 1 ff.[1] I think J. H. Michael is right in translating the
last part of ii, 12 : ' Work out your common salvation in
reverence for one another ' (' fear and trembling ' means
' respect ' [cf. Eph. vi, 5], for Paul cannot have meant that
slaves were actually to tremble before their masters), ' for it
is God who produces in you both the desire and the power
to achieve good will ' (cf. Luke ii, 14).   This exposition
saves us from the un-Pauline phrase ' work out your own
salvation.'   The letter sheds a good deal of light on Paul's
character, but that falls to be dealt with in the next chapter.

The Pastoral Epistles.

Most scholars have long recognized that the two Epistles
to Timothy and the one to Titus cannot have been written

[1] See p. 91.

as they stand by Paul, unless he had changed out of all recognition. The letters have considerable merits of their own, but they are pervaded by a conservative spirit desperately afraid of novelties ; their eloquence is heavy and resounding, not vivacious and discursive, like Paul's. On the other hand, there are genuine Pauline fragments embedded in them, and they can be easily sorted out ; this has been done with great insight and thoroughness in Harrison's famous commentary on the Epistles. The many personal references in Second Timothy cannot have been invented, and the instruction to Timothy to bring ' the cloak, which I left behind me at Carpus's house, and the manuscripts, especially my personal memoranda, (2 Tim. iv, 13), sounds authentic. So does the reference to Timothy's bouts of indigestion (1 Tim. v, 23), though the textual evidence is doubtful here. The passage of which we can be absolutely sure is Paul's dying testament (2 Tim. iv, 5 ff.); I hope to quote part of it in the next chapter.

It seems likely that, after Paul's death, his friends Timothy, Titus, and possibly Luke made a collection of Pauline notes sent at various times to his younger helpers, and worked them up as a manual for young missionaries ; this we possess in the ' Pastoral ' Epistles.

I fancy that the same thing was done for Peter in Second Peter, and that there too we have one or two authentic fragments, worked up with matter of a different kind.

CHAPTER V

THE MAN AND THE SAINT

In the ' Acts of Paul ' (about A.D. 100) he is described as 'a man little of stature, thin-haired upon the head, crooked in the legs, sturdy, with eyebrows joining, and nose somewhat hooked, but full of grace, for sometimes he appeared like a man, and sometimes he had the face of an angel.' The writer is evidently making the best of a bad business, and his description, though laboriously qualified, is so un-flattering that it may be accepted as authentic. Hints in the Epistles and in the Acts justify us in agreeing that Paul was little. At Athens they called him ' this cock-sparrow,' at Lystra they mistook him for Hermes, while the more dignified Barnabas was taken for Zeus. Hermes was a vivacious god, sometimes described as small of stature ; Paul was Hermes, because ' he did the talking.' At Corinth critics suggested that his ' personal appearance ' was ' unimpressive.'

On the other hand, it is clear that there must have been something unusual about his eyes. They may have been weak, for Luke tells us that he had the habit of peering at you (Acts xiii, 9), but as the same thing is said of Peter (Acts iii, 4), we cannot make too much of this. However, Gal. iv, 15 does suggest that there was something wrong with Paul's eyes when he first appeared in the Galatian towns ; ' you would have torn out your eyes for me,' seems to mean more than our common expression, 'I would have given my eyes for so and so.' Of course, we may say that the refer-ence is to his stoning at Lystra, and, if he appeared at

Derbe with a bandage round his head, his hearers might well conclude that his eyes were giving him trouble. But the tradition that Paul suffered from ophthalmia is perhaps too strong to be altogether ignored. After his conversion he was blind for three days and nights; then ' scales ' fell from his eyes at the touch of Ananias. We may, if we like, guess that his eyes were never so strong again.

What was ' the stake in the flesh ' ? Probably the tradition that he was subject to epileptic fits is a superstition, invented in the first instance by Paul's detractors. Julius Caesar, Napoleon, and other great figures of history have been credited with the same disability; in each case the canard has been widely accepted, because it was instinctively felt that there was something uncanny about the man. One who was subject to epileptic fits could not possibly have undergone the superhuman physical and mental strain which Paul bore for years. On the other hand, the suggestion that ' the stake in the flesh ' was simply migraine does not do justice to Paul's description of it; most people who have done much study suffer from it, and it certainly does not incapacitate the victim, though it affects the eyes and is often accompanied not only by a splitting headache, but also by nausea. But no reasonably stoical victim would dream of giving nervous sick headache so imposing a name as ' a stake in the flesh.'

The most likely explanation is that put forward by Sir William Ramsay; it was a kind of malaria, contracted on Paul's travels (he says in 2 Cor. xii, 7 ' there was *given* me a stake '—it was something new). There is a kind of malarial fever which is accompanied by severe headache, described to me by the victim of it as ' like a red hot needle driven into the right temple.' Unlike migraine, it is really prostrating, and it too affects the sight. Paul says in Gal. iv, 14 'you did not spit at the sight of me.'   Malaria is regarded by the natives of Asia Minor as a kind of demon possession, and, like other superstitious people, they spit—to avert the evil omen—at sight of an unlucky object.   On the whole, we may conclude that this was Paul's trouble.   The fact that Luke, who was a doctor, never mentions it suggests that Paul made little of it.

We should think of him as a sturdy little man, bow-legged, with hair rapidly thinning on the top, exceedingly vivacious and talkative, with a tendency to become inarticulate when excited.   We get the impression of a vivid personality, easily taking the centre of the stage in any company in which he was present, perhaps a better talker than listener, but, anyhow, a born leader.   With this liveliness there went a deep reserve ; he was the kind of man who finds it easier to expose his private hopes and fears in a letter than in speech.   He could never have been, like his Master, 'a friend of publicans and sinners,' though he would have made an excellent father-confessor.   He did not, apparently, talk much about his deeper thoughts, for Luke, his companion and faithful friend at the time when he was writing his great Epistles, shows little or no trace of having ever heard of them.   Paul did not wear his heart on his sleeve.

He was obviously every inch a gentleman, as people of his own class noticed at once.   In the most humiliating circumstances, in the midst of a mob ready to lynch him if they could but lay hands on him, in the dock with chains on his wrists, there was no mistaking his dignity.   Festus can only conclude that 'his learning has gone to his brain,' and the Roman officer, who a moment ago mistook him for a revolutionary leader wanted by the police, recognized him as his superior the moment he opens his mouth.

There is a significant note in Acts xix, 31, to the effect that 'the Asiarchs' (at Ephesus) 'were friendly' to Paul; they were actually officials of the imperial religion which, twenty-five years later, has become the 'beast' of the Apocalypse!

With this dignity of bearing, there went a sturdy independence, and a dislike of taking favours from anybody. This is manifest enough in the Corinthian letters, but it peeps out also when he loved his people well enough to take presents, as he did from the Philippians; even then it went a little against the grain. He carries off his embarrassment by a great display of business-like precision. Like many people who have no taste for finance, when he sets out to talk like an accountant, he overdoes it. 'You yourselves know, Philippians, that, when I first began my mission in Europe, no Church kept any debit and credit account with me except you alone, for, even so early as the time when I was in Thessalonica, you supplied what I wanted more than once. Not that I am keen upon your giving me something, but I am anxious for compound interest in your account. Now I can say "Received with thanks," and I have a balance at the bank' (Phil. iv, 16 ff.). Clearly Paul is a little uneasy about the whole business, and is carrying off a delicate situation by working in all the business words he can think of. Some of us understand just how he felt. He did not like taking money, and yet it seemed ungracious to refuse it. I sometimes wonder if he would have had so much trouble at Corinth, if he had not insisted so strongly on his independence! In this matter he was unlike his Master, and sometimes seems to be half-conscious of the fact. Perhaps one of the last things his long experience taught him was how to take money gracefully.

I do not think he was a naturally ' clubbable ' person—
I can find no better word to express what I mean.   He was
friendly, but friendliness and sociability are not the same
thing.   No one except his enemies called him by a pet
name ;   that is surprising, inasmuch as Christians did call
each other by pet names, Priscilla for Prisca, Silas for
Silvanus, Apollos for Apollonius, Epaphras for Epaphroditus, and so on.   Paul was not the kind of person you could
treat in that way ;   it was not that you did not love him
enough to do so, or that he would have resented it, but you
just could not do it.   Wherever he was, he could never be
just one of the others ;   he always held the floor.

Perhaps all but a few of his friends were secretly a little
afraid of him.   He had, we may be sure, a flaming wit in
speech as he certainly had in writing, and his ' come-back,'
as the Americans have it, could be devastating.   Listen to
him when he is in a fighting mood, and notice the sudden
thrust which leaves his opponents gasping.   ' You put
up with it,' he says, ' if a man domineers over you,
if he lives at your expense and is always taking collec-
tions, if he gives himself airs, if he slaps you in the face.   I
apologize that I am, as you say, too much of a " weakling "
to behave like this ' (2 Cor. xi, 20 f.).

' In what, pray,' he says in another place, ' have you been
treated worse than the other Churches, except that I would
not live at your expense ;   forgive me this terrible wrong ! '
One longer passage has been referred to already, but deserves
complete quotation.   ' You see,' he says, ' I don't want to
be " frightening " you, as you call it, by letters.   My
opponent says " His letters are powerful and strong, but his
personality is weak and his delivery too bad for words."
Let the man I mean make up his mind to this, that he will
find me when I do come along in fact what my letters have

shown me to be in theory. Of course I do not venture to compare or class myself with some of these self-advertisers; I judge myself by my own standards, and class myself with people of my own sort!' (2 Cor. x, 9 ff.). Again: 'I am afraid that, when I come, I may find you not the kind of people I want to see . . . and you may find me *very far from being* the kind of Paul you want to see' (2 Cor. xii, 20). Truly he had a sharp tongue, and knew how to use it!

When he is in a less angry mood his playful wit is charming. He liked punning, on the name 'Onesimus,' for instance, or on 'Epaphroditus.' The name Epaphroditus comes from Aphrodite, the goddess of love, and Aphrodite was the name of the lucky throw of the dice, as 'the dogs' was the unlucky throw. Epaphroditus, says Paul, 'gambled with his life, and it was an Aphrodite throw, for he won' (Phil. ii, 30). His epigrams flash out from the pages of his letters everywhere; we may quote a few of them not mentioned already, 'in all things He works along with us for good when we love God' (Rom. viii, 28): 'When I am weak, then I am strong' (2 Cor. xii, 10) with its counterpart 'God's power finds its full expression in man's weakness' (2 Cor. xii, 9): 'Children ought not to put by for their parents, but parents for children, and I will most gladly spend and be spent up for your sakes; but am I loved the less the more I love you?' (2 Cor. xii, 14 f.): 'The letter kills, the spirit gives life' (2 Cor. iii, 6). Here is a cascade of epigrams: 'At every turn we are in distress, never overwhelmed with trouble; in a desperate condition, never in despair, beset by foes, never without a friend, thrown to the ground, but always rising to fight again' (2 Cor. iv, 8 ff.) or again 'branded as deceivers by men, certified by God as true, dying, and, see, we are more alive than ever, under discipline, yet never disciplined to death, sorrowing, yet always

rejoicing, poor ourselves, making many rich, having
nothing, and possessing everything ' (2 Cor. vi, 8 ff.).
Perhaps, however, the most moving of all Paul's epigrams is
to be found in 2 Cor. xi, 29 : ' Who is weak, and I do not
feel weak too ? Who gets upset, and I do not burn with
indignation ? ' It is a perfect description of the pastoral
heart, as memorable in its own way as ' Faith set in motion
by love ' (Gal. v, 6) and ' Love which is the link which binds
the best of all lives together ' (Col. iii, 14). We get the impression that such trenchant sentences were natural to Paul,
when he had got moving. He was often a slow starter, and
labours heavily, when his emotion is deepest ; once he has
got under weigh, each darting sentence suggests another
more pointed still.

Paul's fertility in coining new words like ' over-conquer-
ors,' ' less than the least of all saints,' and specially in the
piling up of superlatives (good examples can be found in
Eph. iii, 19-21 and 2 Cor. v, 17) has often been brought
out. Here we may mention the breadth and variety of his
secular interests. He finds illustrations in grafting (though
he makes a bad blunder here) and agriculture generally, law-
court, slave-market, triumphal processions, racing and
boxing, dice-throwing, potter's shed and builder's yard,
street hoardings, the soldier's armour ; all is grist which
comes to his mill, and his writings are rich in technical
terms like ' first instalment,' 'testimonial ' and so on—
many have been mentioned in other connexions. Paul was
no recluse, no puritan ; he could watch a boxing contest or
a foot-race in the arena with as much appreciation as any
Greek ; he enjoyed the stir of town life to the full, and his
only mistakes in the use of his illustrations occur when he
brings in country pursuits. How eagerly he turns from the
farm to the building in 1 Cor. iii, 9 !

With his flashing wit (for he is as witty as His Master was humorous) and his gusto for active life, we ought to mention the shrewdness of his knowledge of human nature. A searching test of a man's ability to handle others is the kind of collection-appeal which he makes when he has to deal with people who, he knows, are not too generous. Paul has to face a situation like this when he makes his appeal to the Church at Corinth, and we have the whole schemes quite frankly set before us in 2 Cor. viii and ix. He knew the Corinthians were good at talking about things, so he got them *talking* about the collection first. Then he went to the poorer, but much more generous, Churches of Macedonia and said : ' The Corinthians have taken up the scheme enthusiastically ; what are you going to do about it ? ' They took up a collection at once, and it was, as Paul expected, a very generous one. Then he wrote to Corinth, and said, ' You started this business, and so you are responsible for it ; you know how much better off you are than these Macedonian Churches, and your enthusiasm in beginning to talk about this scheme a year ago kindled them. See what they have raised ; you, who are responsible for their sacrificial giving, cannot for very shame fail to do your part.' And in order to see that they did so, he sent Macedonians to take the collection ! There is nothing underhand about this scheming, for he is quite candid about it. Indeed, he tells the Corinthians that it is a fair exchange ; the Macedonians have the grace, the Corinthians the money (2 Cor. viii, 14) ; they have contributed the grace, now let the Corinthians weigh in with the money ! What amazing outspokenness, and what cleverness ! One can almost sympathize with those at Corinth who found Paul sometimes just a shade too clever !

Above everything, this man is alive, on fire with a kind of

explosive energy which still burns on in these letters in which he lives for ever.   His touch is least sure on sex-questions ; perhaps sex-feeling had been left out of his composition, though I cannot be sure of this.   He regards his own freedom from sexual desire as a ' spiritual gift ' (1 Cor. vii, 7); he takes no pride in it, but says that he was made like that, and was glad that he had been, but others had equally valuable gifts.   Some will think that so passionate a soul as he cannot have been altogether indifferent to this greatest but one of all human interests.   We may, if we will, infer that in his case sex had been sublimated ; all I can say is that, by all the tests that I can apply, there is no evidence that Paul had ever been troubled by it.   He is of course painfully interested in sex ; no one who lived at Corinth for eighteen months could possibly for a single day ignore it.   But he is interested from the outside ; he does not really see why people should be so bothered by it, and his consequent inability really to understand women as he understood men is the only serious flaw I can find in Paul's efficiency as missionary and pastor.

There is, I think, ample evidence that he grew and mellowed as he loved and suffered on.   The Paul who quarrelled with Peter and Barnabas may have been a little overbearing at times.   The Acts gives us a picture of this Paul, and his very likeable tendency to let Roman magistrates beat him, and only then let them know that they had no business to have done so, his stage management, so that his ' I told you so ' on the shipwrecked boat has its full dramatic effect, endear him to us.   Roman magistrates were only too ready to think that a beating more or less would do no harm to these pestilent Jews, and Paul was not averse from giving them a salutary shock.   How eagerly he turns from the wooden-minded Festus to the debonair

L

Agrippa, who at least professed to be interested in religion :
' King Agrippa, believest thou the prophets ; I know that
thou believest ! ' But alas ! Agrippa is getting bored, and
says ' In short—to put the matter in a nutshell—you want
me—me !—to play Christian.' ' Yes,' answers Paul, like a
flash, ' the short and the long of it is that I could pray to
God that not only you, but all who hear me to-day, might
become what I am—of course I don't mean stand in the dock
with me ' (Acts xxvi, 27 ff.). Paul has not had much opportunity of preaching lately, and here he is, making a congre-
gation out of a stolid Roman magistrate, a cynical and
frivolous Agrippa and Bernice (if only Paul had known it,
Bernice was the most likely convert of the three, but he
had no eyes for her).

Equally lively is his encounter with the ruffianly high
priest Ananias. When he begins his defence before the
Sanhedrin this brute tells one of the attendants to slap Paul
over the mouth. Whereupon Paul loses his temper, and
we like him for it—it was a dastardly thing to do—and says,
' God shall smite thee, thou whitewashed wall ' (cf. Matt.
xxiii, 27), and God did, as Josephus tells us. Someone says
to Paul ' Revilest thou God's high priest ? ' and he politely
answers, ' I did not know, brethren, that he was the high
priest.' Beneath the courteous apology there is a sting ;
no one would have thought that Ananias was a high priest
to look at him ! However Paul's trials may have mellowed
him, they had evidently not robbed him of his spirit. How
he must have suffered on the voyage to Rome, if he was
really a bad sailor ! But he takes charge of the proceedings,
and to all intents and purposes is captain of the ship before
the voyage is over. And when they land at Malta, hungry
and cold and altogether forlorn, he is busy helping to build
a fire for his companions in distress !

But there can be little doubt that Paul did become more tolerant during those years in Ephesus. He passes from ' If any one of us or an angel from Heaven preaches a gospel different from that which we preached, a curse upon him ! ' (Gal. i, 8) ; and ' If any one will not love the Lord, a curse upon him ! ' (1 Cor. xvi, 22), to ' What does it matter ! as long as in one way or another, as a pretext for ulterior designs or in truth, Christ is preached ; even in this I rejoice' (Phil. i, 18). There is a difference between the ardent young prophet who denounced Elymas and the ' veteran in the service ' who begged Philemon ' for love's sake ' to let him 'get the better of a bargain ' for once (Philem. 20). The change can be defined as coming between the Third and Fourth letter to Corinth.

His desperate adventures at Ephesus, his long imprison-ments, his humiliating experience with the Church at Corinth, perhaps the fact that he owed his life to a woman friend, made him not a more heroic man—he could not be that—certainly a humbler one. He had been ' initiated into the secret ' in everything and with everybody ' to be master of myself ' (Phil. iv, 12), even of his independent temper, his last vestiges of wounded pride. That had been his danger ; it is no accident that the word ' boast ' comes sixty-six times in his letters. Not only did he buffet his body, but he was for ever lashing that pride of his. The repetition of ' What a fool I am !' in the heart-broken letter is surely a deliberate humiliation of himself. He is fighting his last struggle with his sensitiveness, and, when the conflict is over, it is gone, burnt out in the fire of his suffering. What a catalogue of humiliations and agonies, physical and mental, it had been ! It need not be repeated here (2 Cor. xi, 23 ff.). But all this might have made him prouder still, if it had not been for his relentless dealing with himself, his determination to give himself no ease, till Paul had faded out of the picture, and only Christ was left for anybody to see.

All that is left is to ask ourselves, ' What was it, then, which carried this sensitive man with his difficult temperament and ailing body through it all ? ' He tells us about this, as he tells us about everything else ; it was nothing else but love to Christ.   It is doubtful whether Paul made as many converts in his whole ministry as Wesley made in a year or two ; certainly the great world took but little notice of him, and Christian literature in the centuries which followed, while it could not ignore him, proves that neither the Church of his own day nor that of succeeding generations really understood him.   The Christianity which conquered the world was indeed not Pauline ; it was a compromise, and it won the world by incorporating alien elements of which it has not yet entirely rid itself.   But, as Harnack said, his posthumous influence has been like the man himself, a volcanic ferment rising every now and again to destroy the shelters in which the organized Church takes refuge, and force her out into deep waters again.   But all this was hidden from him ; his ambition was not to found so many Churches, much less to turn the world upside down (we make too much of a sentence in Acts ' These men who have turned the world upside down have come here too ' [Acts xvii, 6]—it simply means ' who are making themselves a general nuisance') or make Corinth a place fit for Christians to live in, but simply to ' share the sufferings of Christ,' that is, so to preach Christ that when he saw Him at last, he might not be too much ashamed.   It is strangely true that the men who have changed this world have been other-worldly men and women whose hearts were in Heaven.

Perhaps we can get somewhere near the soul of the man,

if we think of his three great words ' love,' ' gospel,' ' in
Christ.' ' Grace ' might be included among them, for its
use is quite as characteristic of Paul's writing, but it was not
his own invention, as the others were.   ' Love '—it is
not an adequate translation of ' agape,' but I cannot find a
better—was not used as a noun even by Jesus, except in one
passage, the wording of which is doubtful, for Matthew is
quite different here (Luke xi, 42).   In writings outside the
New Testament, it is used in an entirely different sense ;
this is true even of the Septuagint translation of the Old
Testament.   It would seem to have almost disappeared
from contemporary Greek ; in the vast papyrus literature
of the period it has only been traced once, and then in a
decidedly doubtful reconstruction.   Paul took this word
and (in 1 Cor. xiii) made it what it has become, and the same
is true of ' gospel.'   In contemporary Greek it meant ' the
reward paid to the bringer of good news ' ; its comparative
frequency in Mark's Gospel is regarded by most scholars
(rightly, I think) as a sign of Pauline influence ; even Luke
only once uses the noun, and that in a speech of Paul's
(Acts xx, 24).   The last expression ' in Christ ' is the com-
monest of all, and comes in what seem to us rather inappro-
priate places.   Indeed, many interpreters have suggested
that it simply means ' Christian.'   But to Paul it always
meant more than that.

His life was inspired and maintained to the end by a
romance, not the romance of Paul's love for Christ, but
that of Christ's love for Paul.   He never thought of himself
as working for Christ, but of Christ working in him, never
to use the phrase in fashionable evangelical circles, ' bringing
men and women to Christ,' but of Christ drawing people to
Himself through him.   We may be sure that 1 Cor. xiii
is not a picture of saintly living, even though that is what he

may have set out to make it ; it becomes a portrait of Jesus by a lover. All Paul had to do was to tell the ' good news ' ; he was simply a voice, 'as though God were pleading through us ' (2 Cor. v, 20). He was a voice, an ambassador, a bill-poster, anything you like ; but the sooner you stopped thinking about the messenger, and paid heed to the message, the better for everybody concerned. The love of Christ had caught him up into Paradise ; he had been crucified with Him, had carried his little cross of failure and frustration till it rested under the shadow of his Master's great Cross, and had been borne through his agony of shame in the arms of the crucified, had heard Him say, as the waters closed over His head ' To-day thou shalt be with Me in Paradise ' (Gal. ii, 20, 2 Cor. xii, 2 ff.). So he was living in a new world, for ' if any one is in Christ, the whole world is new ' (2 Cor. v, 17). Paul uses ' in Christ ' so often because every detail of his life, his colleagues, his own moods of hope and fear, everything, everybody about him, is ' in Christ,' Christ is the light in which he sees everything and every one. So those troublesome Corinthians are ' saints ' ; when we have read the letters to Corinth and digested their contents, perhaps we shall find that the most amazing words in the correspondence are ' to the local Church of God in Corinth, *consecrated* in Christ Jesus ' (1 Cor. i, 2). Paul evidently means it seriously when he says they are ' called to be saints.' That is how he saw them, and that was why he could never wash his hands of them, whatever happened.

So we come to the end. He had said, ' To die is sheer gain ' (Phil. i, 21) ; ' to be present in this body is to be absent from the Lord ' ; ' if my life is to be my last sacrifice, I am glad and congratulate you all upon the sacrificial ministry of your faith ' (2 Cor. v, 6 ; Phil. ii, 17 f.). At last the summons came : ' For I am already being offered, and the time of my furlough has come ; I have fought the good fight, I have finished the course, I have kept faith ' (2 Tim. iv, 6 f.).

> O ! May I triumph so
> When all my warfare's past,
> And, dying, find my latest foe
> Under my feet at last !

Paul was great as a missionary, great as a theologian and pastor, greatest as a lover of his Lord, for 'the greatest of these' is love.   We do wrong to ourselves and to God's people when we build our life upon anything but sheer love for Christ, and preach anything in the world but His love for us.

'GOD AND LIFE' SERIES

CROWN 8VO.   CLOTH   3s. 6d. each net

A PORTRAIT OF PAUL

By J. ALEXANDER FINDLAY, M.A., D.D.

In this book we have a really valuable 'introduction' to the study of St. Paul's life and work, a book in which a great amount of accurate and careful scholarship is skilfully concealed ; so that while the book should be useful to the student (for Dr. Findlay discusses most of the 'difficulties' and nearly always his comments, translations or paraphrases are illuminating), yet it is one that the 'general reader' could easily enjoy.   His pages on the Corinthian Epistles may be remarked as especially good—*The Times Literary Supplement*.

LIBERAL PURITANISM

By A. W. HARRISON, M.C., B.A., B.Sc., D.D.

Beginning with the Montanists of the second century, Dr. Harrison traces his subject through the Franciscans, the Lollards (this capable essay is by his wife), Milton, with an interesting discussion of the poet's views on divorce, Cromwell, the Wesleyan Revival, to R. L. Stevenson, and concludes with an essay on the philosophy of D. H. Lawrence, who 'reacted against puritanism with all the violence of an overwrought personality.'   Altogether an interesting and able book. —*The Times Literary Supplement*.

THE PRESENT MESSAGE OF THE PARABLES

Some Suggestions as to their Bearing on Present-day Life

By ROBERT E. ROBERTS, D.D.

We have never before read anything written by Dr. Roberts. But he has made us long for more.   For he writes with understanding and with liveliness of the parables.   He takes the well-known stories and makes them speak of to-day, and of us all.   There is a freshness of treatment in this work.   It is so near to life, so well illustrated, and so full of insight.   Many sermons will be born in the minds of those who read this book.   It will be of great value to preachers and teachers, and to all who read it.—*The Methodist Times and Leader*.

THE EPWORTH PRESS (EDGAR C. BARTON)

25-35 CITY ROAD, LONDON, E.C.1

'*GOD AND LIFE*' SERIES

CROWN 8VO.   CLOTH   3s. 6d. each net

INTERPRETERS OF LIFE
By
ROBERT STRONG, M.A., B.Litt.

Interpreters of Life, by Robert Strong, is the work of a religious man looking through a wide range of our literature—Bunyan, Donne, Blake, Christina Rossetti, Bridges, T. S. Eliot are some of the names. Some of the essays, notably that on Donne, show an accurate literary judgement and a wise appreciation of life's problems.—*The Times Literary Supplement*.

WHAT I BELIEVE

A Symposium by forty-two eminent Ministers and Laymen
With an Introduction by the Editor
(Rev. B. AQUILA BARBER)

Thoughtful and sincere, these statements of belief cannot fail to prove of great worth in an age of doubt. Here souls are laid bare and the reader is able to see how these men are able to face up to life's manifold duties and problems. It is a great thing simply and sincerely to set down what one believes.

THE HEAVENLY OCTAVE
A STUDY OF THE BEATITUDES
By
FRANK W. BOREHAM, D.D.

Expositions in Dr. Boreham's most vivid and characteristic style.

They open up in a new and informative manner the teaching of the Beatitudes. It is a book that preachers, teachers and all Christian workers will find most helpful.

THE EPWORTH PRESS (EDGAR C. BARTON)
25-35 CITY ROAD, LONDON, E.C.1

'GOD AND LIFE' SERIES

CROWN 8VO.　　　　CLOTH　　　　3s. 6d. each net

METHODIST GOOD COMPANIONS
By
G. ELSIE HARRISON, B.A

There is wide and accurate knowledge underlying these fascinating studies of prominent old-time Methodists. Mrs. Harrison gives us a touching and sympathetic study of John Wesley's ill-fated love affair with Grace Murray, and a vigorous account of that intriguing character, Dr. Jabez Bunting. We anticipate that the lively and original chapter on ' Reactions in Haworth Parsonage ' will delight Methodist readers and will cause a fluttering of surprise in Brontë circles.

HAVE FAITH IN GOD
By NORMAN H. SNAITH, M.A. (Oxon.)
Senior Kennicott Hebrew Scholar 1925

Interpretations of the spiritual experience of various sacred writers, chiefly Psalmists.

THE WHITE PATH
SKETCHES AND STORIES
By MARGARET DOREEN HADDON
FOREWORD
By ARTHUR PORRITT (Editor of the *Christian World*)
With sketch of Author by B. AQUILA BARBER

This charming book deals with both life and God. Fine and tender work is this. Not unakin to Mary Webb in her power to suggest a close intimacy with the secret of Nature.

DO THE TEN COMMANDMENTS STAND TO-DAY ?
By J. PARTON MILUM, B.Sc., PH.D.

' An excellent treatment of this subject.'—*Expository Times*.
' Nor for long have we read so fresh a treatment of the Ten Commandments . . . a most timely book.'—*British Weekly*.

THE EPWORTH PRESS (EDGAR C. BARTON)
25-35 CITY ROAD, LONDON, E.C.1